CONTEMPORARY MARKETING MIX FOR THE DIGITAL ERA

Nik Tehrani, Ph.D.

authorHOUSE®

AuthorHouse™
1663 Liberty Drive, Suite 200
Bloomington, IN 47403
www.authorhouse.com
Phone: 1-800-839-8640

First published by AuthorHouse   4/29/2009

ISBN: 978-1-4389-3875-2 (sc)

Printed in the United States of America
Bloomington, Indiana

This book is printed on acid-free paper.

I dedicate this book to the true loves of my life, my two daughters, Natasha and Natalia. In addition, I am thankful to my parents, for being the foundation of my strength in life.

ABOUT THE AUTHOR

 Majid Nikanjam Tehrani (Nik Tehrani) teaches E-Business Technology, Management, and Marketing courses at the University of California, Berkeley extension, California State University - East Bay, and Northwestern Polytechnic University in Fremont, CA. He earned his PhD in Business Administration with a specialization in Electronic Commerce from Northcentral University, holds an MBA with a specialization in Executive Management from Pepperdine University and a BS in Electrical Engineering.

Dr. Tehrani is also the Global Director of Program Management at Sanmina-SCI, a leading EMS provider focused on delivering complete end-to-end manufacturing capabilities and highly complex solutions to technology companies around the world. Prior to Sanmina-SCI, he was the managing director and founder of Majital Solutions in Fremont, CA; VP of Sales and Engineering of ACI in Hayward, CA; and VP of Operations of CoMan Manufacturing, Inc. in San Jose, CA.

Dr. Tehrani has taught Management, E-Marketing and IT related classes at Oulu Polytechnic University in Oulu, Finland; Shanxi Administrative University in Tai Yuan, China; Universidad Del Pacifico in Santiago, Chile; and Austin College in Vancouver, Canada as well.

For more information about the author, please visit
www.niktehrani.com.

ACKNOWLEDGEMENTS

Many individuals helped me create this book. I wish to acknowledge all my students at the following schools from 2003 through 2008 for their participation in several ways and providing me with wonderful feedback on the 11 Ps.

University of California – Berkeley
California State University – East Bay
Northwestern Polytechnic University

There are too many students to name, but special mention goes to Ms. Beiyan Yi from Northwestern Polytechnic University and Mr. Paul C. Jones from University of California, Berkeley Extension. My thanks go to you all.

I have the highest praise and thanks to all my mentors and colleagues at Northcentral University and Northwestern Polytechnic University, especially Dr. George Hsieh, President of Northwestern Polytechnic University for his continuous support.

Special thanks to my colleagues in India, Ms. Minita P. Sinha and Mr. Barada Panigrahy for providing me with some market data and case studies.

I would also like to thank Azad Assadipour, a long-time friend, for his contribution to the second edition of this book. His thorough editing has helped to better convey my messages and made significant overall improvement to the book.

TABLE OF CONTENTS

About the Author 3

Acknowledgements 5

Preface 9

Chapter 1
Introduction 11

Chapter 2
People 34

Chapter 3
Internet Product 54

Chapter 4
Partnership 80

Chapter 5
Productivity 105

Chapter 6
Price 124

Chapter 7
Place 146

Chapter 8
Promotion 170

Chapter 9
Personalization 201

Chapter 10
Physical Image.. 224

Chapter 11
Protocol.. 244

Chapter 12
Privacy 262

Chapter 13
Conclusion.. 286

PREFACE

Why <u>Contemporary Marketing Mix for the Digital Era</u>?

Dr. Tehrani adeptly points out the limitations of the traditional 4 Ps (Product, Price, Place and Promotion) that have been followed by the marketers. As the marketing environment changes, there is a need to change conventional marketing strategies. In the same manner that service marketing added three more Ps – People, Process and Physical evidence to the existing 4 Ps to create an absolute marketing mix, a similar change is required in the present day marketing. With the present day marketing going digital, the very concept of conducting business has changed where consumers hold more balance of power. This means, consumers have an edge over the organizations where their demand for better products at lower prices rules. Hence, the additional 7 Ps – People, Partnership, Productivity, Personalization, Physical image, Protocols, and Privacy, are to be adopted by all marketers to meet the changing demands of consumers and survive the competition.

How is <u>Contemporary Marketing Mix for the Digital Era</u> structured?

This book covers the concepts of each of the 11 Ps with up-to-date case studies and examples across the world. It is structured around thirteen self contained chapters. In each chapter Dr. Tehrani explains the necessity of expanding the traditional 4Ps in a simple and organized manner with case studies, laying emphasis on the digital and information technologies that clearly covers the whole concept in each chapter and gives more insight to readers. Furthermore, the author provides the main objectives of each chapter along with a chapter summary. To reinforce readers' understanding on key concepts, all chapters end with a few concept-related questions.

Who is this book for?

This book was written as the core textbook for e-marketing professionals, industry practitioners, academicians, and students who would like to sharpen their marketing skills and keep up with the latest trends in the marketing field. As a result, the Contemporary Marketing Mix for the Digital Era will support students pursuing a master degree in e-commerce, e-business, or e-marketing, MBA, Certificate in Management or a Diploma in Management, as well as undergraduate students in business programs including modules or electives in e-business or e-marketing.

CHAPTER 1

INTRODUCTION

Chapter Contents

- Objectives
- Introduction to E-Marketing
- Definitions
- Importance of E-Marketing
- E-Marketing's Relation to E-Business
- The Internet and E-Marketing
- How E-Marketing is Different than Traditional Marketing
- Benefits of E-Marketing Over Traditional Marketing
- The Evolution of E-Marketing (the dot-com boom/fall/recoup)
- The Present and Future of E-Marketing
- Planning in E-Marketing
- E-Strategy
- E-Business Models
- E-Marketing Performance Metrics
- E-Marketing Marketing Mix
- Use of 4 Ps in E-Marketing
- Limitations of 4 Ps in E-Marketing
- Adding 7 more Ps in E-Marketing (to complete modern day marketing mix)
- Better Marketing Information Systems with 11 Ps
- Security Concerns and Issues
- Security of Organization's, Customer's Database
- Ethical Issues
- Legal Issues

- Chapter Summary
- Review Questions
- References

OBJECTIVES

The objective of this chapter is to introduce to readers the basic concept of e-marketing by giving its meaning and definition, understanding its importance, how it is related to e-business, and the difference between the Internet and e-marketing. An emphasis is placed on making readers understand how e-marketing is different from traditional marketing; the extra benefits of e-marketing over the traditional marketing; the history and evolution of e-marketing, and understanding its present and future.

Chapter one consists of three sections. The first section serves as an introduction to e-marketing. The second section covers the planning aspect of e-marketing, which includes strategy, business models, and the various performance metrics of marketing as it occurs through the medium of electronics. In the third section, the marketing mix -- i.e. how the traditional 4Ps are used in e-marketing, what limitations they pose, how the additional 7 Ps are required to complete the modern-day e-marketing mix, and ultimately how these 11 Ps together help properly market products through effective and efficient Marketing Information Systems.

As organizations get more exposure through e-marketing, they require better security measures. This is one of the biggest concerns, especially for organizations that conduct business primarily through online channels. Proper measures, such as how to secure customers database, address the ethical and legal issues, are where the 11th P – Privacy -- comes into the picture for e-marketing.

INTRODUCTION TO E-MARKETING

Marketing has been in this world since the time humans first traded. It would be fair to say marketing has come a long way since fire-starting twigs and food were traded. Improvement and changes in marketing methods have resulted in efficient marketing strategies including audience targeting and effectively getting marketing messages across. It is imperative for businesses to achieve a competitive edge in today's marketing environment. The concepts of venerable marketing principles applied with the modern communication technologies have made it not only possible, but much easier to deliver value to customers while managing the relationship with them, benefiting both the organization and the stakeholders. This dawn, in short, has been termed as 'e-marketing'.

DEFINITIONS

E-Marketing[1]: an integral part of e-business activities, is an abbreviation for electronic marketing and is referred to as *online marketing* or *Internet marketing*. It is defined, in simple terms, as the marketing of products and services over the Internet i.e. our goal is marketing a brand[2] and we are achieving the marketing objectives through the use of electronic communication technology.

As defined in the book *E-Marketing*, by Strauss, Ansary, and Frost[3], the application of information technologies in a broad range for –

1 http://en.wikipedia.org/wiki/Internet_marketing
2 http://www.quirk.biz/resources/88/What-is-eMarketing-and-how-is-it-better-than-traditional-marketing
3 E-marketing, 3rd Edition, Judy Strauss, Adel El-Ansary and Raymond Frost, Prentice Hall, 2003

- Creating customer value by bringing changes in the marketing strategies like focusing on the segmentation, targeting the appropriate market, making differentiation and positioning the product rightly.

- Efficiently planning and executing the new ideas; competently supplying, promoting and pricing of products or services.

- Satisfying the needs of individual/organizational customers by creating gain to everyone in the value chain.

- The use[4] of electronic media such as the internet, *wireless marketing*, and *iTV* for any marketing purpose. _

The Ohio State University[5] website in its glossary defines e-marketing as –

> …Moving elements of marketing strategies and activities to a computerized, networked environment -- such as the Internet. It is the strategic process of creating, distributing, promoting, and pricing goods and services to a target market over the Internet or through digital tools.

IMPORTANCE OF E-MARKETING

E-Marketing has become important in today's marketing field due to its certain characteristics, such as allowing for more effective and efficient marketing strategies and tactical implementation. It has been changing the concept of marketing by shifting power from sellers to buyers; eliminating geographical distance as a concern; allowing

---

4 http://wps.pearsoned.co.uk/wps/media/objects/1452/1487687/glossary/glossary.html#E

5 http://aede.osu.edu/Programs/e-agbiz/pageglossary/main.html

communication regardless of time zones; enabling greater collection, storage, and analysis on customer information; emphasizing an interdisciplinary focus, giving importance to each and every discipline related to marketing; and using intellectual capital as a more important resource than financial capital.

E-Marketing is an automation device that helps an organization to identify its most valuable prospects as well as customers, convert them into a fruitful business opportunity, help them grow, and keep them as loyalist throughout a lifetime for continuous future business growth. The marketing methods that help in this process include banner advertising, e-mail marketing, online customer behavior analysis, lead generation, and campaign management.

At the Kellogg School of Management, Philip Kotler[6] emphasized that it is important for marketers to understand technology and respond to the new forces of today's economy as digitalization and the Internet are becoming the major sources of efficiency and profitability among companies. Managing the information in an intelligent way along with the use of technology-supported customer interactions is among the e-marketing techniques for the new economy. It is very beneficial for an organization to endeavor in becoming electronic and paperless, and forming partnership with its customers, suppliers and distributors for a win-win strategy.

The Internet has resulted in more intense competition, proliferation of channels and different media, globalization, and price reduction of

---

6 http://www.kellogg.northwestern.edu/news/hits/011105cw.htm (New economy calls for new marketing)

goods and services through e-commerce. There are various benefits[7] an organization gains through e-marketing, some of which include:

- faster cycle time
- higher response rates
- improved lead management
- simplified campaign testing

Though the biggest challenge organizations are facing is the integration of e-marketing with their existing marketing methods and activities, it is paramount that organizations take steps that help them to meet this challenge. The integration of e-marketing should take care of the Customer Relationship Management (CRM) software, databases, and back-end systems. One has to understand that e-marketing is an end result of a succession, over time, of marketers wanting to better reach and serve their clients. Identifying, targeting, and constantly interacting with buyers through e-marketing help to blossom businesses over a 3 – 4 year range, thus facilitating growth and value of the digital market places, ensuring e-marketing's place as an avenue of growth of both CRM and e-CRM. Procter & Gamble, for example, coped with hard times by setting up a dashboard for its marketing managers that allowed them to access template processes, best practices, testing tools, scripts, industry news, and project dates.

E-MARKETING'S RELATION TO E-BUSINESS

E-Business is a term coined by IBM in the 1990s. As per Gartner Group: e-business is a continuous optimization of a firm's business activities through digital technology i.e. through the use of computers and the Internet. E-Business helps any organization focus on proper and potential customers as well as the trade associates and retains them.

---

7 http://www.allbusiness.com/marketing-advertising/4283264-1.html

There are different e-business markets, for example Business to Business (B2B), Business to Consumer (B2C), and Business to Government (B2G). The business, consumer, and government sectors can be in different combinations as per the initiations taken by each one of groups i.e. if a consumer initiates the request then it could be C2B, C2C, and C2G. If government initiates the request then the relationship is G2B, G2C, and G2G. In general, most e-businesses occur in the B2C and B2B markets, followed by the B2G and C2C markets.

E-Businesses focus on transactions through a subset called **E-Commerce**. A further subset of e-commerce is e-marketing where the information technology is largely applied to traditional marketing practices. Information Technology (IT) is applied in the processes of creating, communicating, and delivering value to customers, and for managing customer relationships in ways that benefit the organization and its stakeholders.

THE INTERNET AND E-MARKETING

Internet marketing is very significant to today's businesses. There are companies, such as e-Bay, that are gaining 100% of their revenue through online business. A majority of customer service requests are being fulfilled online without much dependence on the traditional methods of customer service such as online banking services. The Internet is basically a network of interconnected networks of millions of computers where the individual computers of different organizations, government, corporate, private entities hold webpages in a global environment providing accessibility to others who are in the network. These computers use Internet Protocol to communicate with each other where the data is moved over phone lines, cables and satellites. The U.S. Department of Defense invented[8] the Internet for the Advanced Research Projects Agency (ARPA) in the late 1960's. As per the U.S. Department of Defense's estimate, there are more than 2 billion websites with more than 600 million Internet users worldwide, and these numbers are swiftly increasing.

There are three technical roles played by Internet:

1. Content providers create information, entertainment, etc. that resides on computers with network access.
2. Gives users (client computers) access to contents and e-mails over the network.
3. Provides an infrastructure to move, create, and view contents (hardware and software).

Internet marketing uses the Internet as its base along with various technologies like Internet media and other digital media such as wireless mobile media, cable, and satellite. With the help of this medium, Internet marketing has been able to achieve the classic marketing objectives while sustaining the contemporary marketing theory.

Dave Chaffey[9] shows a difference between the Internet marketing and e-marketing by defining Internet marketing as "Achieving marketing objectives through applying digital technologies." According to Chaffey, it is not the adoption of technology that should determine investment in Internet marketing, but the results delivered by that technology. The technology includes Internet media such as websites

8   http://www.udel.edu/interlit/chapter1.html#growth
9   http://www.davechaffey.com/Internet-Marketing/C1-Introduction/E-marketing-Internet-markeitng-%20definition

and e-mail, however, other digital media like wireless/mobile, cable, and satellite should not be overlooked.

Though e-marketing is equivalent to Internet marketing, e-marketing has a wider scope as it does not refer to just the digital media, but also includes management of digital customer data and electronic customer relationship management systems (E-CRM systems).

E-Marketing makes use of some of the non-web Internet services like e-mail and internet related newsgroups as a valuable pathway for marketing purpose and reaching the actual target. Hence, it is much bigger than the Internet with a reach far beyond the web. In fact, e-marketing predates the web as many e-marketing technologies exist as used in Electronic Data Interchange arrangements, Customer Relationship Management, Supply Chain Management, etc.

HOW E-MARKETING IS DIFFERENT FROM TRADITIONAL MARKETING

The application of information technology in traditional marketing concepts results in e-marketing. E-Marketing affects traditional marketing in two ways. Firstly, the efficiency and effectiveness of traditional marketing functions increases with e-marketing. Secondly, many marketing strategies are transformed with the technology of e-marketing, resulting in new business models and adding value to customers.

BENEFITS OF E-MARKETING OVER TRADITIONAL MARKETING

Compared to traditional marketing, many advantages are provided through the use of e-marketing. Especially with the change of time and competition, there has been a fundamental change in marketing, it happened with buyers having the balance of power in their hands. The blogs, online bulletin boards, chat-rooms, and other online communication channels have made marketers practically losing control over their brand images.

The emergence of e-marketing has made the world a global village without distance. Geographic location is no longer a factor for collaborating with business partners, supply chain organizations, customers, or just chatting with business associates and friends in any corner of the world. Thus many businesses have realized the need to eliminate barriers.

The concept of 8-hour work days or 9AM– 5PM business hours has vanished with the arrival of e-marketing. The time has been totally compressed which was a hurdle between firms and their stakeholders/ customers. There are online stores that are open 24/7 with various products available under one roof. People have the convenience of self-service ordering and tracking with added facility to communicate per the convenience of their own time schedule with least preference given to the time zones of different countries. The Internet has created the avenue for a timeless and borderless marketing field.

E-Marketing has made it easy for customers and/or potential customers to access and gather the required information at the lowest cost. Furthermore, e-marketing has made it easier to get a marketing message out into the "hands" of a broader customer base. People can also store pertinent information for comparison with other competitive products thus enabling them to make their own decisions for future purchases at their leisure. There are other benefits of e-marketing:

1. Drastically reducing the cost of communication. For example, one can send effective customized e-mails to mass customer listings or other stakeholders at a lower cost.

2. Reducing the cost of inventory, product distribution and transaction processing.

3. Adding value to products/services by providing online Frequently Asked Questions (FAQs) service and customer support.

4. Cost savings due to less labor required.

5. Creating a paperless environment through electronic order processing and communicating with customers directly. All the latest Enterprise Resource Planning (ERP) packages offer this benefit. Though the initial set-up cost involved is high because of costly hardware/software, training, and maintenance, it still works out to be more profitable in the long run provided proper strategies are developed and implemented with a viable business model.

6. Helping an organization to reach new markets, thus increasing customer base, building customer relationship and customer loyalty apart from helping the company acquire knowledge at lower costs through research and customer feedback.

7. The cascading effects of all of the above reduce costs, and thus decreasing the overall cost of customer service.

THE EVOLUTION OF E-MARKETING

In the mid-nineties some existing well-established organizations, along with most of the new dot-com companies, made their presence on the web. All had high hopes of attracting huge sales and gaining the largest market share possible. Unfortunately, because of a speculative bubble[10] (also referred to as IT bubble/dot-com bubble) that made these organizations look over their standard business models and focus more on increasing market share at the cost of their profits, very few of them were successful. The gloom was almost 7 years long, from 1995 to 2001, beginning a relatively mild and lengthy recession in the developed world. Within a span of three years, from 2000 to 2003, more than 500 Internet firms shut down in the United States alone. Even with such failure, the traditional established organizations felt that the internet technologies that they had used in their dot-com business had changed the basic structure of their industry. The marketers developed an inquisitiveness to gain knowledge insight into which specific technologies would help them in increasing their sales and profitability. Such interest has grown and brought e-marketing to its existing stage today.

THE PRESENT AND FUTURE OF E-MARKETING

Presently:

Because of the use of information technology by marketers in their marketing practices, there has been an intense and tremendous response from people to the art of e-marketing communication that were otherwise immune to the traditional marketing practices and strategies. E-Marketing has changed the way marketing is conducted.

Marketers are able to reach people via the Internet in a better way[11] than they would have done with telephone, television, snail mail, or other communication medias. E-Marketing has eased the reach of marketers to their target audience and helped them sell in an efficient and effective way.

---

10 http://en.wikipedia.org/wiki/Dot-com_bubble
11 E-marketing, 3rd Edition, Judy Strauss, Adel El-Ansary and Raymond Frost, Prentice Hall, 2003

In the Future:

E-Marketing is here to stay with a bright future[12] provided it is properly integrated into the existing marketing strategies. Properly used it presents bigger opportunities for companies. Marketing on the Internet has split the market where the marketers are forced to create products and messages geared to even small target groups. Andy Petro, Director of Marketing, Eclipse Inc.,[13] says to produce the desired results, the Internet marketing groups should be kept with the corporate marketing groups. On the other hand, futurist Tim Mack[14] predicts that dishonest marketing may get worst as there are both cooperation and competition on the Internet. Moreover, e-marketers tend to choose highly competitive strategies over cooperative ones because of their short-term thinking. Even the involvement from government will increase as the evidence that company ethics does not exist on the web with more deceitful online sales practices.

Marketers should also be aware of another implication of the Internet – i.e. the information overload which is both a good and bad situation – good because there is an infinite amount of information accessible to customers; and bad because customers may get confused with such a large amount of information.

PLANNING IN E-MARKETING

Planning is the first basic management principle that needs to be followed by any organization. Proper planning helps an organization to make a profit at a low cost and have a sustainable business with competitive advantage, thus allowing for the development and

---

12 http://www.bwa.org/notes/nov01BWA.htm
13 A Boulder company that provides software to distributors to automate their business processes
14 http://www.ired.com/news/2000/0010/emarketing.htm

maintenance of a viable fit between its objectives, skills, resources, and changing market opportunities. Planning helps organizations to apply digital data and information technology both effectively and efficiently. It also helps the organizations to have a clear vision which can be translated through the marketing process from e-business objectives and strategies into e-marketing goals. Well-planned and executed strategies and tactics play a vital role in achieving those goals. The planning process in e-marketing involves creating an e-marketing plan, implementation of the plan, evaluation of the plan, and taking corrective action where needed.

E-STRATEGY

Strategy is the means to achieve goals and objectives set by a firm. It is the process of deciding what detailed plans a firm is going to use to accomplish its goals. Strategies exist at different levels in an organization's marketing plan. Each functional area of a firm develops its own strategies to help achieve the overall client's objectives. When an organization deploys an enterprise resource to capitalize on technologies to achieve its objectives, such situation is known as **E-Strategy** i.e. the organization uses information technology components such as the Internet, digital data, databases, etc., in its business strategies. Thus we can say that e-strategy or e-business strategy is the addition of information technology to corporate strategy.

E-BUSINESS MODELS

Any successful organization follows a certain method of doing business in order to sustain itself in the market and make profits. This particular method is referred to as a model. Thus, the model which is used for doing business is called a business model. When we apply information technology in any of the business models used by organizations, it is known as **E-Business Model**. The e-business model adopted by a company should not only be profitable to the organization but add value proposition for its partners, customers, and other stakeholders.

E-MARKETING PERFORMANCE METRICS

Any action that is measured helps us to understand past performance. Similarly, Performance Metrics for e-marketing helps in knowing whether the company has reached its objectives. This is computed by means of measuring the effectiveness and efficiency of an organization's operations, thus helping the organization to make any adjustments or corrections to ensure they are well on track to accomplish their original goals. There are various systems through which performance can be measured. For example, the well known measurement systems include Six Sigma and Balance Score Card.

E-MARKETING MARKETING MIX

The traditional marketing mix consists of 4 Ps – Product, Price, Place, and Promotion that are applicable to products sold[15] over the counter. With the prevalence of the Internet, the way businesses are conducted have changed -- customers are purchasing online after doing thorough research on competitive products, -- hence the traditional 4 Ps need to be expanded. Accordingly, organizations change their strategies and make them suitable to the environment attracting and retaining more customers.

USE OF THE 4 Ps IN E-MARKETING

Akin to the strategies adopted by the marketers in providing the right product at the right place while doing the right promotion at the

---

15 http://www.learnmarketing.net/emarketing.htm

right price, e-marketers need to use similar marketing mix to achieve the desired objectives. As a product, in terms of e-marketing, can be intangible and physically not present, marketers need to create an attraction by giving detailed facts, features, and specifications about the product online, providing pictures of the product from various angles along with online customer support for handling any immediate inquiries.

Similarly, e-marketing involves online purchase without any particular place for a certain transaction or any mediator. Customers deal directly with the manufacturer. Companies must ensure that products are delivered on time apart from ensuring that its site is easily accessible and clearly visible on other sites when advertised.

Online trading helps customers get more bang for the buck as they are able to take advantage of built-in discounts because distribution costs, staff costs and warehouse costs are reduced thus allowing pricing to become more competitive. Consequently, consumers have the power to compare and purchase products online that offer them the most competitive pricing. At times, customers prefer online auctions for a bargain. All of these options are made available to customers with the ease of the Internet, along with added safe payment methods through credit or debit card or direct debit from their bank account (e-check).

Because of this easy access and easy payment, promoting a product right is again an important task. High visibility is needed and can be achieved. Having a recognizable domain, using webpage links and/ or placing banner advertisements on other sites where your potential customers browse, are some of the effective tools in increasing visibility. Organizations need to manage web-oriented public relations as well.

Strategically placing important news[16] on your home site and other sites, conducting e-mail campaign, etc., on a continuous basis, will aid in the successful marketing of your products.

LIMITATIONS OF 4 Ps IN E-MARKETING

The 4 Ps of e-marketing are a set of marketing tools which an organization uses to pursue its marketing objectives in the target market. If e-marketing is to be successful, its prerequisites include connecting with customers and serving their needs apart from accomplishing the stated mission of the organization. A successful e-marketing process creates value through customer satisfaction from brand building before the sale is even takes place to post-sale service and support. The 4 Ps are the broad groups of the marketing mix concept introduced by E Jerome McCarthy in 1960. The implementation of the 4 Ps evolved from the selling point of view. The 4 Ps of marketing support B2C[17] marketing, but when it comes to managing the marketing and selling of complex B2B products and service-based solutions, they become irrelevant.

7 MORE Ps

As seen above, the traditional 4 Ps that are applied in the e-marketing concept have certain limitations. Hence, there is a need for additional Ps for sustainable growth of an organization in this competitive world. Seven more Ps are identified apart from the existing ones in order to complete the dynamic marketing mix of e-marketing. They are People, Partnership, Productivity, Personalization, Physical Image, Protocols, and Privacy.

---

16   http://www.learnmarketing.net/emarketing.htm
17   http://first.emeraldinsight.com/marketing/articles/4ps.htm?PHPSESSID=1423 baeb156c88436a 5b112cb723626c

1. People

People, in an organization, means both the internal (employees) and the external (actual) customers. An organization needs to identify the requirements of both the internal and external customers for a cordial and profitable future.

2. Partnership

An organization needs to maintain an effective relationship with its stakeholders – both suppliers and distributors (forward alliance and backward alliance) in the value chain to maintain good logistics and supply chain.

3. Productivity

Productivity is the amount of output produced with a given input. Productivity must be continuously maintained and improved by marketers through studying various changes such as socio-cultural, technological, and economic events in the market place.

4. Personalization

Personalization plays an important role in offering services online. Personalization can be achieved by proper interactions with customers, setting and analyzing their profiles and data, and following appropriate marketing strategies.

5. Physical Image

The design of your website should be in a way that attracts visitors at the first visit. Not only the design, but the functionality of a website needs to be very simple including easy navigation and easy transaction processing, such as order booking, tracking and/or payments.

6. <u>Protocol</u>

A website is somewhat uncontrollable when used by the people across the world. A website must be vigilant of the laws of different countries. The web designers should keep this rule in mind while taking care to remember the Standard Operating Procedures (SOPs), mechanisms, localization, legal systems, the cultural and linguistic relationship flows.

7. <u>Privacy</u>

This is the last but the most important aspect of the e-marketing mix. Customers' database consists of sensitive and important personal information such as bank account numbers, credit card numbers, date of birth, social security number, etc. Such information must be kept confidential to avoid any online frauds. Any mismanagement in confidentiality of customer information will adversely affect the business. Further in-depth discussions of the 7 added Ps follow in subsequent chapters.

BETTER MARKETING INFORMATION SYSTEMS WITH 11 Ps

Marketing Information Systems[18] (MIS) is a system through which a business can track various actions of its customers from the time they visit their website until they leave. This is possible through some computer programs which can either be simple as spreadsheets, or be complex like sales forecasting tools designed to track customer activities. MIS helps businesses know what their customers are buying, what their likes and dislikes are and the services they prefer from a particular website.

---

18 http://www.e-com.sbdc.com.au/e-marketing/general/glossary.htm#m

With the help of all 11 Ps, covering all the aspects of e-marketing, it becomes a much easier and more achievable task for marketers to gather information on customers' and other stakeholders' needs and activities. Ironically in numerology, number 11 is a powerful number which represents high ideals and balance[19]. It reflects a perfect balance between various objects. The number 11 is observed as two straight lines side by side which symbolizes that although separate, they are one individual value and image. Along these lines, the 11 Ps in the e-marketing mix are separate entities. However, when taken together, the 11 Ps are the true power behind the success of e-business. At the end of the day, both e-businesses and traditional businesses must be better equipped to offer products and services to all the target groups that would reach the level of delight going beyond the step of customer satisfaction.

SECURITY CONCERNS AND ISSUES

People using digital technology are prone to online security threats and cyber crimes in the form of misuse of customers' sensitive and confidential information, creating financial and other possible loss to them. Hence, e-marketers need to pay special attention to the confidentiality[20] aspect. Similarly, integrity becomes another important issue. The integrity of the website and the business must ensure that data between the sender and the receiver will not be misused. Lastly, availability of resources is another concern where customers should have the right to access the resources that are meant for them.

---

19   http://tribes.tribe.net/4f953607-b038-4291-a7d3-1d82ef338bec/
thread/9301a771-ed66-47aa-8986-20bebf129981
20   http://www.ibm.com/developerworks/websphere/library/techarticles/0504_
mckegney/0504_mc kegney.html

SECURITY OF ORGANIZATIONS AND CUSTOMER DATABASE

An organization should not only be concerned about the online security of itself, but also the security of its customers. There are instances where banking websites are replicated by the criminally-minded seeking vital information about customers and that information being misused causing customers financial loss. Similarly, **Phishing** is another form of trap being used to gather confidential data about customers. Phishing is the criminally fraudulent process of attempting to acquire sensitive information such as usernames, passwords, and credit card numbers, expiration dates, etc. by means of masquerading as a trustworthy entity via an electronic communication channel. Although various security measures have been enforced by means of user authentication, authorization, encryption, and auditing, unfortunately they do not guarantee a totally secure system. All organizations must be concerned about the various ethical and legal issues while developing their e-marketing strategies. Site security is a lifelong and ever-changing concern that cannot be overlooked.

ETHICAL ISSUES

Ethics relates to the values professionals hold and the practices they follow, as well as their concerns towards the society as a whole. There are various codes of ethics established for online marketing in an attempt to conduct fair dealing and transactions. But it is undeniable that a long-term e-business must choose to only use customers' and potential customers' sensitive data in an ethical manner.

LEGAL ISSUES

Legal issues come into the picture when addressing the concerns of people in a certain country. The most important ethical and legal concerns are issues related to data collection and usage of sensitive, otherwise private data. Other concerns are spams, product and industry criticisms, and certain morally and legally unaccepted expressions that are sometimes directed towards children. Other emerging legal and ethical issues are jurisdiction, fraud and online governance.

CHAPTER SUMMARY

E-Marketing is the marketing of products and services using digital and electronic communication technologies. It helps to create customer value by bringing changes in marketing strategies, plans and execution of new ideas, and ultimately improve customer satisfaction.

E-Marketing is closely related to e-business as e-marketing is a sub-set of e-business while it is larger than the Internet with a wider scope as it uses even non-web Internet services for marketing avenues. E-Marketing enhances traditional marketing with the addition of information technology to existing marketing strategies, thereby cutting down costs to companies and increasing the benefits to customers.

Even after a strong downfall of dot-com companies, industry has seen a benefit in digital technology and when properly used and integrated into the existing marketing strategies, e-marketing brings a brighter future for an organization. Planning is an important aspect of e-marketing. An organization with proper planning that uses e-strategy in their e-business models will certainly thrive. Success of organizational operations can be measured through performance metrics systems. An e-marketer must be concerned about the online security of the organization as well as the customers where issues related to ethical and legal aspects should be fairly dealt with.

For e-marketing to be successful, additional 7 Ps are added to the traditional 4 Ps which have been used for decades in marketing. These 11 Ps altogether help e-marketers to gather proper marketing information that help them strategize accordingly for future growth. Chapter 2 focuses on the first P – People, which is the foundation of any successful business.

REVIEW QUESTIONS

1. Define e-marketing and what is its importance?
2. How do you compare e-marketing with e-business, the Internet, and traditional marketing?
3. Discuss, in brief, the evolution, present and future of e-marketing?
4. What is the importance of planning in e-marketing?
5. What are the limitations of the 4 Ps in e-marketing and how do other Ps suffice these limitations?
6. What are the various security concerns an e-marketing organization should focus on and why?

REFERENCES

1. http://tribes.tribe.net/4f953607-b038-4291-a7d3-1d82ef338bec/thread/9301a771- ed66-47aa-8986-20bebf129981
2. http://www.whats-your-sign.cspiritualmeaningofnumbereleven.html

CHAPTER 2

PEOPLE

Chapter Contents

- Objectives
- Introduction
- External Customers
- Internal Customers
- Case Study: Seagate's E-Procurement Initiative
- Chapter Review
- Review Questions
- References

OBJECTIVES

Chapter two focuses on the customers of Internet business. It highlights both internal and external customers and explain the importance of satisfying the varying needs of different customers. This chapter further discusses the importance of customer relationship management systems, which are designed and implemented to improve the understanding of customer preferences and needs. Additionally, this chapter introduces e-procurement systems and explain how they are used to achieve total customer satisfaction. The chapter concludes with a case study on the e-procurement initiative by the Seagate Company, a leading company in storage technology.

INTRODUCTION

The 1990s witnessed rapid technological advancements that revolutionized the way businesses are conducted. The technological advancements have brought the world closer and led businesses to consider all world markets irrespective of their own geographical presence in these markets. The prevalence of the Internet and other associated technologies on the web have enabled businesses to market and sell their products over the Internet, not just as an extension of their geographical presence, but also as a pure online player.

Most businesses have similar consumer themes, and can be grouped into the following broad categories:
- Extend business presence using the Internet
- Make use of existing infrastructure investments
- Reduce costs of securing, servicing, and retaining customers
- Enhance customers' overall experience
- Improve business intelligence

- Collaborate existing systems and strategies with other companies to complement business strengths
- Create a centrally managed security mode

The advancement of the Internet has dramatically affected the ways in which businesses can operate. The Internet has opened up new communication channels, new opportunities, new ways to connect to suppliers and customers, and the possibility to personalize communication based on customer needs. Companies are constantly thinking of ways to effectively connect to customers and stakeholders. However, businesses in the digital realm have yet to define the meaning of the term 'customer'. Traditionally, a customer is the person or entity who ultimately uses a product or service. At the same time, businesses also deal with external agents who provide the inputs for business operations. The delivery of these inputs is significant because it determines the quality of the output. For this reason, these external agents, or suppliers and vendors, can be treated as customers internal to the company.

For a business to thrive, it needs to focus on providing customer satisfaction. The very basic premise of customer satisfaction is to understand the needs of customers and deliver the product that matches or exceeds the customer's expectations. Businesses, in their pursuit of customer satisfaction, often implement strategies that are generally directed towards the external or end customers, while the suppliers/vendors (internal customers) are totally neglected. However, if businesses can satisfy their internal customers, which means the process of input flow is smooth, the output delivery can be maintained to the expected level of the end customers. Therefore, total customer satisfaction involves appeasing both internal and external customers.

In addition, successful businesses must understand the market that they want to cater to as well. Many times businesses fail even when they provide high quality products/services whereas failing to meet the specific demands of customers – the products they make and the customers they cater to do not correlate. To appropriately understand the market, businesses must first identify their customers and then identify their needs. Once the customers are identified, it is important to assess the needs of the target customers and ensure that their products or services meet the needs of their target customers. However, given the variability of consumer needs and preferences, businesses must constantly monitor their assessments on the needs and preferences of their target consumers. Those who successfully adapt to the changing needs and preferences of their consumers are able to build long-term business relationships that improve their prospects for long-term business success. This is not only true for businesses that operate in the 'real world', but also for those who only operate in the 'virtual world'.

The general principles for being successful in Internet marketing are similar to traditional marketing methods. The difference is that the Internet has drastically changed the paradigms in which businesses can interact with their customers and other stakeholders. In this new marketing environment, marketers need to incorporate the traditional principles of marketing with new strategies that take into account new innovations, the changing business environment, and new social values. These three considerations will determine the course and direction of any business's success in marketing an e-business.

CHAPTER 2

EXTERNAL CUSTOMERS

To deliver the right product to the market, marketers must understand their target market, its demographics, needs, socio-economic conditions, and purchasing behavior. This understanding will not only result in better product/service delivery, but also help to establish a set of loyal customers that will be vital to the long-term success of the business. Customer insight helps marketers to integrate the information into various aspects of business. This is not just true in the case of markets, products or services, but also applies to interacting with vendors and suppliers.

Effective marketing on the Internet requires effective research tools, concept building, revisions of objectives, perseverance, and the ability in calculated risk-taking. It is essential to use research tools to understand consumer needs and preferences. These research findings must then be incorporated into the business's marketing strategy for both short-term and long-term growth and success. In addition to monitoring consumers' needs and satisfying the customers, Internet businesses need to optimize costs while providing the best quality of service. With the correct combination of unique product/service offerings and superior quality of service, profitability can be achieved even in the highly competitive global environment. Moreover, it plays a vital role in staying ahead of the competition.

An e-business has both online and offline customers. The very first step to reaching out to these prospective customers is to network and create interactions. This is possible through utilizing electronic communication such as promotional newsletters and emails, but not overlooking more traditional promotional methods. Once the target market is identified, initial interaction is achieved, and a small amount of sales is conducted, then the business must ensure that their initial customers are satisfied with the quality of their products. This will allow the business to generate repeat sales and establish a customer base going forward.

Another way to encourage repeat customers is to impress them with the web presence of the company. The online shopping experience should be positive, user-friendly, and simple. The goal is to persuade customers to make repeated visits and ensure their satisfaction every time they visit and shop. The e-business needs to devote sufficient time and resources for the design of the web-store. The web-store must be up to date with current information on products, services, and promotional offers. In addition, the web-store must be easily navigable for customers, offering them sufficient purchasing options and providing a forum to suggest improvements or leave feedbacks and comments. Any feedback from visitors to a business's website should be monitored carefully and any problems fixed promptly to ensure customer satisfaction.

However, the biggest challenge for marketers is the identification of potential customers. Not all people who use the Internet will be prospective customers to businesses. Hence, marketers must use the services of search engines like Yahoo!, Google, and MSN to identify their prospects based on the search terms frequently used by web browsers. From this research, businesses can direct the identified prospects towards the web-store through emails and other online and off-line promotional techniques, thus drawing potential customers to the web-store. A comprehensive strategy should be developed to engage interested customers, such as those who have clicked on a banner ad, a discount offer, a product catalogue, or even purchased an item. These interested customers in turn will possibly become referrals to bring in more customers. Once the e-business has established a set of loyal customers, the company may then increase prices reasonably as necessary without a fear of losing business. The dedicated customers will most likely forego minor price changes if they believe they are receiving superior quality and service. Over time, the business gains recognition for its products and services and distinguishes itself as a unique brand to the target market.

Therefore, a steady stream of revenue can be reasonably expected if the external customers are satisfied with the quality of product or service they receive. The business can further strengthen and scale up its business by providing effective after-sales service, customer support, and establishing ongoing relationships with its customers.

Businesses are constantly looking for new ways to interact with their customers. Successful businesses collect pertinent information about their customers for the purpose of conducting sales and improving customers' online shopping experiences. These methods of interaction attract customers and improve satisfaction by saving customers' time, making their shopping more convenient, and personalizing their shopping process. The three basic factors in e-business customer identification and satisfaction are time, convenience, and personalized attention.

As people get busier, **time** becomes a crucial factor in choosing what businesses to purchase products from. Customers look for immediate gratification in the form of speedier delivery of products and services. If this is not addressed, the market is competitive enough that customers can easily switch to a business that provides the same quality products and services faster.

Convenience is another important factor to all customers. Customers want their shopping process to be convenient, they can buy the products they want at any time and from any place. In addition, customers need conveniently accessible product information. They are looking for easy access to product comparisons, reviews, and available discounts.

Customers also seek **personalized attention** from online businesses. Therefore, businesses must design their websites to identify each shopper when she visits and recommend products and services that could appeal to the customer based on her previous purchases. Businesses that can effectively give customers personalized attention through their website will harvest the benefit of high customer loyalty.

In the world of Internet businesses, **Customer Relationship Management** (CRM) is considered a crucial area which needs to be focused on and leveraged (Exhibit 1). CRM system helps identify prospective customers, managing current customers and supply partners, and enable employees to respond accurately while minimizing response time and overall cost.

Customer Relationship Management (CRM)

CRM is viewed as a business process environment having three major focus areas. CRM manages communication and contact with a customer wherever the customer touches the organization, in a sales call, support service or any other marketing effort. It attempts to provide the service needed by the customer at the point of time. CRM benefits the organization by:

1. Tracking customer information: It empowers the company to access, update, and monitor information about the customers. It could be a sales enquiry or purchase information.

2. Respond to requests and anticipate needs: CRM helps the sales and customer support teams to respond to needs of the customers.

3. Provide targeted marketing campaigns: Information obtained about customers can help in targeting specific campaigns to different customers.

4. Manage customer-centric activities throughout the company: Valuable customer insight not only helps the sales team and customer support teams, but also other teams across the organization. For instance, it can help the R&D to bring out better products.

Exhibit 1: Customer Relationship Management (CRM)
Source: Harry Breslford, Michael S. Toot, Karishma Kiri, Robin Van Steenburgh, "Internet Solutions – A Need Analysis", Chapter extract from <u>Connecting to Customers</u>, *2002.*

INTERNAL CUSTOMERS

Suppliers and vendors play a very important role in any business organization. Their products and services are the catalyst for business operations and cannot be neglected. They are the internal customers who need to be satisfied through effective systems, procedures, and payments. They, in turn, can keep the external customers satisfied by delivering quality inputs on time. Therefore, the quality of the encounters between the organization and the internal customers influence the quality of delivery of the products/services with the end customers. With technology advancing at a rapid pace, businesses are looking for methods to identify, evaluate and plan for new technologies that can integrate with existing applications and processes. This requires support from various stakeholders in the business, including internal and external customers.

Businesses that have embraced the idea of expanding their business to the Internet have to remodel their business strategies to meet new demands. Many, out of necessity, have implemented applications that procure inputs from suppliers, making it possible that the seller/company can ship directly from the suppliers to their customers. This function helps reduce storage expenses and also better serves the customers through the Internet. There are many benefits derived from e-procurement and e-service. Notably, businesses can reduce costs, communicate more effectively with their suppliers, and greatly increase productivity.

To better serve internal customers, businesses must identify their network of internal customers, their needs, and their expectations. The internal customers' needs and expectations need to be further aligned with the goals of the business. In all markets, successful businesses are those who work closely with their vendors and suppliers and develop strong partnerships. The results of a strong partnership are innovative products and cost reduction (Exhibit 2).

Benefits of Vendor Partnership

A certain travel company was launching a new online system. It required infrastructure upgrade involving several vendors. Initially the company was rigid in issues related to pricing. However, it later realized that project implementation time was a crucial factor. The CIO of the company initiated a more open and relationship-based negotiation with a core team of vendors who were crucial for the project and were of value on a long term basis. This enabled the vendors to become strategic partners for a long term. It also triggered new ideas and insights. The project was completed on schedule and at minimum costs.

Exhibit 2: Benefits of Vendor Partnership
Source: Baljit S. Sail and Andrew S. West, "Building Stronger IT Vender Relationships", http:www.mckinsyquartely.com

In the new era of Internet commerce, companies must focus on collaboration to maintain better relationships with their internal customers. Collaboration takes place in the scheme of everyday transactions. In a transaction, there are three parties involved – 1) the buyer, 2) the seller, and 3) the market creator in the middle. There are three barriers to collaboration for web-based suppliers: trust, adoption, and reasoning.

In some businesses, such as an online bookseller, the business-to-business (B2B) interactions are far simpler. However, in industries involving the purchase of industrial materials and supplies, the sales process is more complex and involves certain mandatory obligations that need to be fulfilled for transactions to take place. **Trust** in the marketplace between businesses and consumers depends on various factors, including readily available information about the product, transparent data, penalties in case of non-delivery, representations and warranties of the product's quality, etc. If businesses have appropriate information and assurances in place, this will ease and expedite the process of creating trusting relationships with customers and collaboration with other businesses.

The second barrier to collaboration for web-based suppliers is **adoption**. When the market creator or the business adopts new software to streamline the ordering process and insists that its suppliers buy and use the same software as well, it may create tension in the business's relationship with its suppliers. Suppliers might not be open to the adoption of new technology for logistic and/or cost reasons or sometimes they might lack the necessary resources. For example, when Wal-Mart issued an ultimatum to its suppliers – requiring them to use RFID tags for their items -- many suppliers were reluctant because of the high cost involved in adding RFID to their businesses.

The last barrier to collaboration for web-based suppliers is **reasoning**. Many times the implementation of new processes and systems on the Internet may lead to various events that must be addressed by the business. Such corrective action could involve compliance with new regulations or the payment of fees. In either case, this corrective action could lead to additional cost to the business. Therefore, businesses must be cautious with new ideas but still continue to develop new technology and new products.

As businesses increasingly shift the focus of their activities to the Internet, the B2B (Business to Business) relationships are being revolutionized. Earlier B2B was an inward-focused activity. It required entry of transactions on a computer screen and coordination through telephone or fax lines. With the Internet's resources in place, B2B interactions have been evolving to a more outward focus. This outward focus reduces inventory costs and labor costs. Additionally, it reduces the time required for the procurement and purchase of supplies and other inputs. These new business processes and technologies have made B2B activity more significant, greatly enhancing the satisfaction levels between businesses and suppliers.

Research has shown that the use of the Internet in procuring inventory from suppliers has added value to the primary activities of the organization and therefore decreased costs and increased profitability. Furthermore, the reduction in delivery time has added significant value to external customers. Thus, effective supplier interactions on the Internet can enhance the overall satisfaction to the end customers. However, it is impossible for companies to maintain strong relationships with all of its suppliers. Therefore, it is prudent for businesses to determine certain ground rules that appropriately distinguish between critical and non-critical suppliers (Exhibit 3).

Vendor Relationships

Companies, generally face the problem of investing resources to maintain strong relationships with its vendors. At this point, it becomes important to separate the critical vendors from the non-critical ones.

A critical vendor is one who provides the main products that support crucial technology or products of the company. They could also be providing services and products that eat away a major chunk of the company budget. These are the vendors who are crucial for the business operations and relationships with them need to be intensified.

Non-critical vendors are the ones who supply standard products that support the production or other activities. Companies try to obtain the products from them at the best price and seek bids from others. With such vendors relationships that are transactional in nature should be enough.

After ranking the vendors, the company should compare the skills of the critical vendors to those of the employees of the functional units. This can help in analyzing how the two complement each other. The company needs to assess what can be achieved with each critical vendor – whether cutting costs, better products, insights of how other competitors are using the same products, etc. Further, the company can also assess the skills and commitment of these vendors and determine which of the vendors have the greatest impact on the company. It is also important that the company considers the vendors who are not with the company at that time. This can open up avenues to forge relationships with new vendors.

Exhibit 3: Vendor Relationships

Source: Baljit S. Dail and Andrew S. West, "Building stronger IT vendor relationships", http://www.mckinsyquarterly.com, June 2005

E-Businesses generally sell and market their products in accordance with traditional marketing principles. However, the rules of these principles are changing as the way of doing business changes. The traditional marketing mix has become an e-marketing mix and has four primary segments: People, Product, Price, and Promotion. This chapter has dealt with one of the P's of e-marketing mix. It discussed the People aspect of marketing which is constituted of customers and suppliers. It also discussed the importance of maintaining the relationship with these customers. Apart from maintaining a good relationship with the people involved in online business, a wide variety of product portfolio is required to function as an effective business. In the next chapter, we will discuss the importance of maintaining a wide range of products by businesses to maintain a competitive edge.

CASE STUDY

SEAGATE'S E-PROCUREMENT INITIATIVE

Seagate, a renowned name in storage technology, was established in 1979. During that time, the company fuelled the PC revolution with its hard disk drives. Two decades later, Seagate is again enabling the growth of the Internet by becoming the world's largest manufacturer of disc drives, magnetic discs, and read-write heads.

In January of 2003, Seagate decided to move from a manual procurement process to an electronic procurement process. It was one of Dell's largest customers in terms of purchasing dollars. Dell had integrated to the Ariba Services Network for e-procurements. Hence

Seagate approached Dell to move to a B2B connection to enable them to purchase Dell products through the Ariba based applications.

However, Seagate faced certain problems while implementing the technology. Usually buyers use the B2B connection by having their suppliers' product information for purchasing into spreadsheets and other file formats. The files are transferred to the customer by e-mail, File Transfer Protocol (FTP) or by faxing the documents. Ariba facilitated the use of Catalog Interchange Format (CIF) for buyers to send their product information electronically. Alternatively, it used catalogs by exporting data from the spreadsheets and uploading the items into the Ariba programs in the CIF format. Dell began e-procurement with Seagate in this manner. This helped the customer to select the items for purchases from the supplier's catalog and order via e-mail, fax, and/or e-Xtensible Markup Language (XML).

Using CIF was advantageous in terms of better purchasing and managing the content of Seagate's online catalog. However, the information of precuts in the catalog was difficult to maintain as spreadsheets. Several other files were transferred back and forth between Seagate and Dell to maintain accuracy and product availability. The Loading of CIF also required employees at both Dell and Seagate to interact. In addition, Dell was unable to provide pictures of third party items with CIF for customers to review products. Furthermore, the product description fields were limited to 256 characters and in spite of the process, Dell had to print the e-mailed purchase order and re-key it into the Dell order system. This was time-consuming and increased the possibility of human errors.

To solve this problem, Seagate adopted a solution, "Punchout" with Dell which was hosted by another Ariba supplier. This new system allowed Seagate end users to shop from Dell's catalog. The program could merge the order requisition into Dell's e-procurement system and submit the order in XML. It additionally could receive an acknowledgement for the purchase order thus confirming each order.

Adopting the Punchout solution solved several problems. 1) The sales team at Dell could update any price or technology change immediately in the catalog. 2) Seagate was relieved of catalog maintenance. The new system was merged with Dell's existing online information. This enabled customers to view current images and product descriptions. Further, no additional resources were required to manage the catalog, thus saving time and the possibility of human errors.

In terms of payment, Seagate used American Express for catalog orders. With Ariba, items purchased by several suppliers were combined into one single payment from the American Express system. Through the e-procurement process, Seagate used the Ariba Order Link numbers to secure purchase orders with the American Express payment system. This helped in speeding up the reconciling process for attaching the purchase orders to the invoices as paid.

Seagate has acknowledged the optimization of its ordering process through the e-procurement system. Punchout helped Seagate shoppers since Dell hosts the catalog, updates, and makes it easy for buyers to access the items. Seagate furthermore has the flexibility to suggest modification to the Dell's team.

Source: "Seagate – B2B Integration Case Study"
http://www.dell.com/content/topics/global.aspx/casestudies/en/2003_
seagate?c=us&l=en&s=gen

CHAPTER REVIEW

The 1990's witnessed a digital revolution. The Internet has dramatically changed how the world communicates. The biggest shift took place when businesses discovered the advantage of moving their businesses online. Many companies offering all kinds of products and services dotted the Internet landscape. However, the dot com burst proved that those with strong business values and sound business strategies would be the only survivors. The businesses with the best success were those who truly valued their customers – both internal and external.

When a business has established a presence on the Internet, end customers have the option to purchase online in addition to shopping in the business's physical stores. Irrespective of how the products are purchased, these customers' needs must be first and foremost understood so that products are designed around these needs. Moreover, it is also important that the needs of the customers are constantly monitored. Businesses must implement an effective customer relationship management system to help gain insight into customers' preferences and tailor products accordingly. This will encourage repeat business, and help build long-term relationships with the customers.

Businesses must invest time and efforts to satisfy their internal customers, i.e. the suppliers and vendors. As business operations have become increasingly easier to manage on the Internet, many companies implemented e-procurement system. This has helped to reduce cost while making transactions with the suppliers and vendors a lot easier and more efficient.

Satisfying internal customers requires establishing long-term relationships with critical vendors. Relationships with vendors, to a great degree, are dependent on trust. Other factors that influence the business's relationship with internal customers include price, negotiating power, product quality, product availability, service, payment, etc.

In conclusion, e-business requires consistence and unity with traditional marketing principles. E-Businesses must also adapt to a new set of rules and considerations. These new considerations are essential to the satisfaction of both internal and external customers.

REVIEW QUESTIONS

1. Discuss the changing paradigm in the wake of companies making a presence on the Internet either for sale or for providing information, etc.?

2. Explain how companies strive to satisfy their external customers? Illustrate with suitable examples.

3. Gap Inc. sells it products online and off-line. How is the company striving to satisfy customers in their stores and in their online shops?

4. What are the constraints in establishing vendor relationships? Discuss.

5. With reference to the case study, how did Dell Inc. help Seagate in implementing the e-procurement system? What were the benefits derived out of this system by Seagate?

REFERENCES

1. Allen Thomason, "*Making your E-customers happy*", http://www.jpservicez-searcharticles.com/.../141645/1/Business/213/Work-Life/Making_your_E-Customers_Happy.

2.   *"How will the Internet change B2B Supply chains?"*, http://
      knowledge.wharton.upenn.edu/article.cfm?articleid=158,
      March 29th 2000

3.   "Seagate – B2B Integration Case Study",
      http://www.dell.com/content/topics/global.aspx/casestudies/
      en/2003_seagate?c=us&l=en&s=gen.

4.   Harry Brelsford, Michael S. Toot, Karishma Kiri, Robin Van
      Steenburgh, *"Internet Solutions – A need Analysis"*, Chapter
      extract from the book, Connecting to Customers, 2002.

5.   *"Creating Value through E-commerce Business Models"*, http://
      knowledge.wharton.upenn.edu/article.cfm?articleid=254,
      September 28, 2000.

6.   *"A B2B Exchange is Born: Will e2open.com Succeed?"* http://
      knowledge.wharton.upenn.edu/article.cfm?articleid=198,
      June 7th, 2000.

7.   Baljit S. Dail and Andrew S. West, *"Building stronger IT vendor
      relationships"*, http://www.mckinsyquarterly.com, June 2005.

8.   Michael Dylan, *"Customer Service Tips for Online Businesses"*,
      http://_www.woopidoo.com/articles/dylan/customers.htm.

INTERNET PRODUCT

Chapter Contents

- Objectives
- Introduction
- Meaning and Definition of Product
- Levels of Products
- New Product Development
- Managing New Products
- Product Life Cycle Strategies
- Product Decisions
- Product Line Decisions
- Product Mix Decisions
- Product Marketing and Information Technology
- Case Study: Google
- Chapter Summary
- Review Questions

OBJECTIVES

The objective of this chapter is to give a basic introduction to the product concept and discuss how it is managed through the Internet. This chapter discusses the different stages of a product, and how they are categorized as core, actual, and augmented level. This chapter also discusses the development process for a new product in the new era of Internet commerce and how the development process is aided by and managed with information technology, how a product's different stages of life cycle can be improved, and what strategies marketers can use to promote, sell and improve the product. Additionally, this chapter addresses various attributes of service offerings, what strategies can be used for services marketing, and how products and services are ultimately distinguished. This chapter also explains how various products related decisions are made with specific reference to product line and product mix.

The role of information technology is significant when it comes to product marketing. Information technology has totally changed the rule of the game in the marketing and selling process. However, businesses should never deviate from standard ethical practices while applying and implementing new methods of Internet product marketing or new uses of technology in their marketing strategies. Ethical values and beliefs play a vital role in the long run for businesses as they develop trusting relationships with the internal and external customers, and create a positive image for the business in the marketplace.

The chapter concludes with a case study on Google's new products, including the unimaginable Google Mobile, featuring considerable new technology and great feedback from end users. The case study shows how technology is used productively to enhance the life of human beings, how the Internet plays an important role in the process, how various costs are reduced due to the benefits conferred upon the customers. The case study explains and demonstrates many product related concepts, such as product levels, product life cycle, branding, and packaging of services, product labeling, and marketing of the overall product using appropriate marketing mix techniques.

INTRODUCTION

In e-commerce, when a customer purchases products through the Internet, these products (or components before finished products) are provided to the seller by the suppliers who are an important part of the people component discussed in chapter two. As discussed previously, both people and product are important components of the e-marketing mix. The people (customers and suppliers) use Internet technology to buy and sell products. The success of an e-business depends on its ability to provide a greater variety of products at competitive prices. This chapter explains how businesses categorize and sell their products over the Internet.

MEANING AND DEFINITION OF PRODUCT

Product means anything that is tangible or intangible, offered for attention[21], acquisition, and use or consumption to meet or satisfy the requirements of a user or consumer. It is a bundle of attributes or benefits packed with value proposition offered by the seller after understanding the needs of the buyer. The buyer, in turn, is willing to pay money or barter other items of value for that product.

---

21 Principles of Marketing, Philip Kotler and Gary Armstrong, Prentice Hall, 12th Edition

Product can also mean an outcome[22] of someone's hard work or of a certain situation. For example, skill is the product of hours of practice; any adverse reaction of a human being can be the product of his hunger and fatigue.

A product can be the result[23] of:

i.   Labor (when a wall is built)

ii.   Thought (when an idea is generated to implement)

iii.   Growth (a growing child having a healthy meal)

iv.   Generation (like mangoes in summer, wine during Christmas)

Knowing the meaning of product is of great application value to marketers as it helps them to understand how consumers[24] are attached to certain products and the way they relate themselves to those products. It helps marketers to predict the responses from consumers, thus aiding in the actual designs of the products. Additionally, it helps explore the manner and extent to which unpleasant earlier experience can predispose future uses.

WHAT IS A PRODUCT?

A product can be any combination of physical or non-physical objects; it can be a service or an event; it can be person, places or organizations; it can be an idea or a mix of ideas, a person, place or organization. Generally, products are divided into the following two categories: 1) Consumer Products and 2) Industrial Products.

22 http://ardictionary.com/Product/12298
23 http://thinkexist.com/dictionary/meaning/product/
24 Journal on Humans in ICT Environments, "Product meaning, affective use evaluation and transfer"; Sacha Helfenstein, Department of Computer Science and Information Systems, University of Jyväskylä, Finland, Volume 1 (1), April 2005, pp 76-100

1. **Consumer Products**: Products that are purchased by an individual for personal consumption. These products are available in B2C and C2C markets.

2. **Industrial Products**: Products that are used as components in the operation of an organization for manufacture into a different final product or for resale (B2B market).

While a product is tangible, a **service** is an intangible form of product consisting of various activities, benefits or satisfactions[25] offered for sale. There is no ownership of anything physically tangible at the end of this entire process. Other characteristics that a service has are –

- A service is labor intensive[26] and cannot be separated from the supplier,
- A service is variable as it is not produced by a single entity before finally passing on to the customer,
- A service is perishable as it cannot be stored for sale or use at later date.

The marketing strategies[27] for services differ from those of the marketing strategies for a physical product, because marketing for services is based on the relationships maintained between seller and customer and the value offered to the customer. Once a service is provided, the buyer cannot return it. In addition, in the field of Service Marketing comparing the quality of similar services is difficult.

---

25 Principles of Marketing, Philip Kotler and Gary Armstrong, Prentice Hall, 12th Edition
26 http://ollie.dcccd.edu/mrkt2370/Chapters/ch5/5service.htm
27 http://en.wikipedia.org/wiki/Services_marketing

LEVELS OF A PRODUCT

A customer purchases available products based on his perceived value of the products. A customer is typically satisfied only when his perceived value is less than or equal to the actual value provided by the product. There are different levels of product that satisfy a customer. These levels are classified into different categories:[28] Core, Actual, and Augmented. Philip Kotler has taken the same product model and divided it into five levels[29] : Core Product, Generic Product, Expected Product, Augmented Product, and Potential Product.

1. Core Product: The actual benefit which a customer sees in the product he purchases. This level of product is intangible as it measures, the customer's benefit. For example, when a customer buys an iPod, he is paying for and benefiting from convenience -- i.e. the ease of listening to music anywhere, anytime, thus satisfying his fundamental need or want.

2. Generic Product: The level of the product that contains only attributes or characteristics that are entirely necessary for the product to function.

3. Expected Product: The set of attributes that buyers normally expect and agree to when they purchase a product.

4. Augmented Product: The supplementary characteristics and benefits that differentiate a product from its competitors.

---

28 http://www.marketingteacher.com/Lessons/lesson_three_levels_of_a_product.htm
29 http://www.provenmodels.com/16/five-product-levels/kotler

5. Potential Product: These are the various potential growth prospects and changes that would happen to a product in the future.

The five levels of products (Figure 1) are not strictly listed in direct order of importance. Some observe that there is more competition at the Augmented Product level than at the Core Product level -- i.e. at the level where additional characteristics and product benefits are provided as compared to the competitors. Therefore, businesses must pay special attention to what customers value highly, such as product storage and packaging, advertising, important customer information, cost, and the planning of product deliveries.

In the new era of Internet commerce, many products are positively impacted by features of the Internet. One unique aspect of the Internet is the availability of search engines. For products like a mobile handset or a DVD, the Internet functions as a new distribution channel, providing potential customers with unique, technology-enabled service.

The above model is a tool for analyzing the relationship between the business and its customers. There is intense competition to attract customers who shop online, causing businesses to use marketing strategies that provide customers value in different forms, including creation of psychological satisfaction in the purchase of the product, positive product experience, and meeting the customer's expectations.

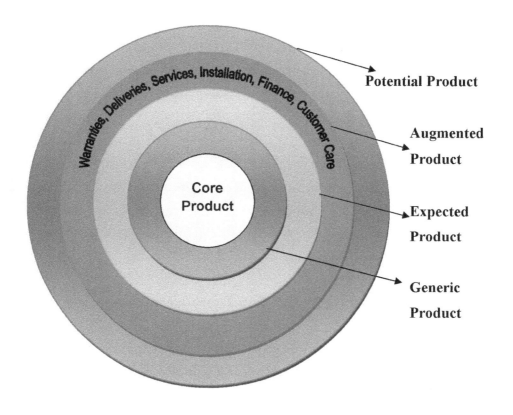

Figure 1: Five Levels of a Product

NEW PRODUCT DEVELOPMENT

For most businesses, long-term survival in the marketplace depends on the successful **Development of New Products and Services**. Products generally do not have a long life span due to changing tastes, rapidly developing technologies and fierce competition. Therefore, products need to be managed properly and replaced more frequently. However, businesses must also be able to quickly recognize which new products are likely going to fail. Otherwise, businesses may misallocate their resources and will not be able to operate effectively. Business survival and growth requires risk-taking in the innovation process. Successful innovation requires both ingenuity and careful planning. When an innovation is backed up by sincere efforts, meticulous planning, and systematic product development process, it will surely lead to success.

A typical new product development process has 9 critical stages. At each stage, the marketer must make decisions as to whether it is still in the best interest of the company to proceed further with development of the new product, or whether changing or abandoning the product is a better option.

The nine stages of New Product Development Process are:

1. **Idea Generation:** Idea generation is a systematic search for new ideas from both internal and external sources of the business. Some important ways of generating new ideas are:
    - i.   Research and development
    - ii. Soliciting customer feedback (through questionnaires, direct meetings, complaint/suggestion boxes, etc)
    - iii. Conducting surveys and focus groups discussions
    - iv. Studying competitors and their products
    - v.   Interacting with members of the distribution channel
    - vi. Referring to print and electronic

media, attending seminars, discussions
with people in the industry and the
academicians

Businesses must choose the right new product to offer to the market. Businesses must ensure that their best ideas reach the market and their inferior ideas do not end up too costly. Developing a new product is difficult, as shown by the fact that 70 – 90 percent of new products launched fail within the first year. These failures can generally be explained by one or more of the following considerations:

- The product's concept may be good, but the market share may have been overestimated;
- Product design has not translated into a high quality finished product
- Positioning in the market was wrong with ineffective advertising
- The product was priced incorrectly for the marketplace
- A product idea reaches the market despite expectations of failure due to the influence of a manager who has made an inaccurate evaluation of the product
- The cost of product development rose beyond expectations
- Competition is exceedingly tough in the market

Therefore, it is important for any business to first understand the needs of the customers, the existing market conditions, and the competition before developing any new product in order to deliver superior value for the target customers and experience overall market success.

2. **Idea Screening:** The idea screening process involves the screening process for new ideas and a business decision to go forward with only the few best ideas for potential new products. Formal written analyses on the new product are prepared, outlining the product's features, recommended pricing, target market, market size, competitors, calculated costs, expected returns, and any other important information. Generally, product development committees are formed and will decide, as a group, what new product ideas have the highest potential for profitability and success.

3. **Concept Development and Testing:** After the best idea is chosen, a concept plan about the product is to be developed in order to offer it to the market. This stage calls for preparation of an exhaustively detailed report of the product idea which consists of the virtual image of the actual product as perceived by the customers. Based on the research findings and analysis, the best product concept is chosen for concept testing.

4. **Concept Testing:** The new product concepts are tested with different groups of target customers before launching the new products to the marketplace. Based on the feedback received from the focus groups,

products are modified as necessary before the product's marketing strategy is implemented.

5. **Marketing Strategy Development:** A suitable marketing strategy is required before introducing the product to the market. The strategy must detail the expected target market, plan how the product will be positioned in the market, what volume of sales is anticipated, what percentage of the market is likely to be captured and what amount of profits are anticipated in the initial years. Additionally, the strategy must outline a plan to price the product competitively, deal with logistical issues, and a yearly marketing budget for promotion of the product.

6. **Business Analysis:** After the development of the marketing strategy, the subject company needs to carry on a business analysis that involves reviewing of projections of sales, costs, and profits. The business uses these projections to determine whether their expectations of the product's overall success will satisfy the basic objectives and needs of the business before proceeding to the next stage of product development.

7. **Product Development:** This stage requires huge investments, as the conceptual product is developed into an actual product by the Research and Engineering team. Coordination with all of the departments involved in the initial stages of product development is important so that the actual product matches the

initial concept plan. The product should be rigorously tested to ensure its safety and performance prior to introducing it to the market.

8. **Test Marketing:** After these initial internal tests confirm that the product is ready for sale, the test marketing must be conducted to see the market's reaction to the newly launched product. Test marketing serves to minimize cost by avoiding huge unnecessary investments in case the product has a very short life cycle. In addition, it helps the business to gauge the effectiveness of its own marketing strategies. Test marketing also helps determine where the business must focus its efforts more on with respect to the new product, such as advertising, positioning, pricing, branding, packaging, and/or strategies.

9. **Commercialization:** Once satisfied with the test marketing, the business proceeds to commercialization of the product, -- i.e. launching the product into the marketplace. This stage is the most costly, because the business must incur the major initial costs of promotions, advertisements, distributions, storage, and working capital.

MANAGING NEW PRODUCTS

Managing New Products[30] is where business can gain or exercise a strategic competitive advantage. For any new product or service to generate profits, a business must integrate its business strategy with the

---

30 http://www.kellogg.northwestern.edu/execed/programs/MKTG07/index.htm

new product design and development. Successful product management requires the business to operate with an innovative mindset in a way that benefits the long-term goals of the business. The managing of new products needs to be frequently monitored to avoid any major deviations from industry standards.

The business must put new products through a Strategic **Auditing** process. This entails an assessment of the past performance of the business during earlier product launches. The business will use these previous experiences to guide their planning for the new product. This could involve better portfolio planning for the new products or implementing better marketing practices used in other industries. What new lessons learned from previous bitter experience will help guide the business towards future innovations. The marketing strategies for new products should be clearly defined and the business should identify whether their strategies are market-driven or if they are using strategies that may end up being a trend setter in the market. Businesses must decide whether they want to stay with the market, or if they want to be first movers in the market. If a business is a late entrant, it will be forced to adopt existing market strategy to establish a solid presence in the market.

The new product needs to be properly segmented and positioned through adopting suitable and effective strategies. There are various segmentation tools and techniques available that can be used by marketers to design an effective marketing plan. Furthermore, businesses need to build cross-functional teams that help manage new products in a more efficient and effective way. With advanced scientific research in this field, there are various teaming techniques, tools, and guidelines that can be followed to help marketers understand the characteristics of the leader, thus enabling team members to form a strong cross-functional team. The process calls for rewarding and motivating those teams that actually perform their marketing duties well and advance the business's goals.

PRODUCT LIFE CYCLE STRATEGIES

All businesses want their new products to have long life cycles in order to generate more profits. If the life cycle of a product is longer, it means that the product remains profitable over a longer period of time and is beneficial to the business. The longer the life cycle of a product, the more sales and the higher profits for the business. A product usually goes through four stages in its life cycle – **Introduction**, **Growth**, **Maturity**, and **Decline**. The product life cycle is graphically represented in Figure 2.

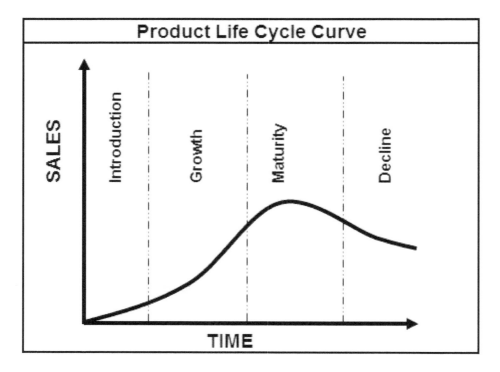

Figure 2: Product Life Cycle Curve

Introduction Stage

The **Introduction Stage** is where sales growth is slow and profit is almost non-existent, as the product has just been newly introduced in the marketplace. Initially, the introduction stage involves significantly high costs. A business must choose a strategy that remains consistent with their intended product positioning. This strategy is the first step in developing a better marketing plan for the total life cycle of the product.

Growth Stage

The **Growth Stage** is predicated on the satisfaction level of the market. In this stage, the product may have been well-received and more significant profits are generated for the business than in the introduction stage. New competitors see the success of the trend-setters in the market and there is more entry, creating a larger market. New market segments are created, adding new distribution channels. With more competitors, prices are usually lowered to attract more buyers, and product conviction is emphasized more than product awareness.

Maturity Stage

The **Maturity Stage** generally lasts longer than the preceding stages. In the Maturity Stage, sales generally slow down and profits decline. This means that the product has largely reached the market and has been accepted by the potential buyers. It is a challenging stage for marketers because it calls for modified marketing strategies to generate more sales. Sources for change in the marketing strategies can include better advertising campaigns, changing product characteristics, price reduction, and aggressive sales promotions.

Decline Stage

In the **Decline Stage**, the sales of the product eventually dips, plunging to zero ultimately. The causes for this stage could be a shift in customers' tastes, increased competition, and/or technological advancements. Businesses must constantly identify products in the decline stage because it is costly and against their interests to continue selling and marketing a product which no longer has any appeal in the market. The business must decide whether to maintain, modify, or drop the product.

PRODUCT DECISIONS

There are certain major product decisions marketers[31] must make to meet the needs of customers in Internet marketing. These include Attributes, Branding, Support Services, and Labeling.

1. **Attributes:** The specific features and overall quality of a product are the product's Attributes. Quality is generally correlated with price — higher quality is expected at higher prices. Specific features of a product include its color, taste, style, size, and speed of service. The Internet offers customers a lot of choices. Customers can select their desired products as per their own customization by personalizing the product that meets their individual requirements.

2. **Branding:** Every product has a brand name or a symbol that is used to identify and differentiate it from those of other competitors. Branded products are patented to protect their trademark from competitors. Branding helps create a relationship with the customers, making the product/service

---

31 E-marketing, Judy Strauss, Adel El Ansary, Raymond Frost, Prentice Hall of India, 2003

a part of their life. It is important for online products to have names that are short, simple, unique, speakable, memorable, and easy to spell. Most online products co-brand with one another to increase their reach.

3. **Support Services:** This is an important marketing decision where providing customer service plays a vital role. Support Services form a crucial part of the Customer Relationship Management for all successful companies. When businesses provide customers with adequate support at each stage of online product purchase, customers' overall shopping experience is greatly enhanced, and customer complaints are minimized.

4. **Labeling:** Labeling helps to identify not only the name of the brand, but also the features of the product and the business responsible for the product. The labeling aspect for online companies includes product usage, product features, and other product related information that is provided on the website.

PRODUCT LINE DECISIONS

A **Product Line** refers to a group of products that are closely related and function in a similar manner. These products are basically sold to the same customer group. Product lines are marketed through the same types of outlets and fall within similar price ranges. There are several Product **Line Decisions** that must be considered, such as the product line length. Product line length refers to the number of items in the product line. A product line is generally considered to be too short if profits can be increased by adding items to the product line. A product line is considered to be too long if profits can be increased by removing items from the product line. A business's objectives and resources influence a product line length. Businesses may want to choose different lengths if they want to get involved in up-selling, cross-selling, or simply to protect themselves against economic swings. A company can fill its product line by adding more items that are generally similar to the present products in the line. This is basically done to utilize excess capacity, plug any holes, satisfy dealers, or to present a product line that is more complete to put the business in a better position in the market against its competitors.

PRODUCT MIX DECISIONS

Product Mix is an assortment of items that consist of all of the product lines that a business offers for sale. Product mix decisions impact the overall size of a business. When a business adds more product lines, they widen the product mix and by virtue increase the overall size of the business. Lengthening the existing product line enables a company to be associated with a full line of products. Businesses can also choose to pursue less product lines if they are limiting their market involvement to one particular line. Either way, the product mix decisions must be consistent and in accordance with the business's strong reputation in a single or several fields.

PRODUCT MARKETING AND INFORMATION TECHNOLOGY

A product will have many new opportunities when it comes to the online environment. Today, e-marketers can make use of a wide variety of technologies that offers substantial support in their product strategies. Powered with the networking and communication strengths of the Internet, e-marketers must capitalize on the Internet's property and technology to deliver the benefits to customers through attributes, branding, support services, and labeling. Some of the technologies that are easily available and are widely used by marketers across the world are:

1. **Websites:** Hyper Text Markup Language (HTML) helps in the construction of websites. There are more simplified programs with the latest additions of HTML forms, dynamic HTML, XHTML and XML. These languages help in developing programs to run on web servers or on the user's browser.

2. **Plug-Ins:** Plug-ins help play multimedia files. Some widely used plug-ins are Real Player, Acrobat, and Flash.

3. **Database Marketing:** Database Marketing is basically used for promotional campaigns where relational databases help to retrieve the required data through query language, among which the most popular ones are SQL, Oracle and DB2.

Marketers should be cautious of computer viruses. Computer viruses can destroy existing information on the computer's hard drive, damage software and/or other important computer programs. Generally, viruses come in through emails and external drives. Businesses must make sure to have the necessary anti-virus software and firewall to protect the important information, prevent any misuse of data, and create a safe up-keeping of the information.

Marketers must realize that the Internet, as a direct marketing medium, increases the overall efficiency of the marketing process.

Information Technology affects the product and brand name strategy as well as implementation. However, if Internet marketing is not utilized in the proper way, it can adversely affect the product's sales.

An e-business is considered successful if it is able to both provide a product at a reasonable price and deliver it to customers on time all over the world. Businesses can expand their global reach by establishing and maintaining partnerships with other organizations in different parts of the world. Such partnerships enable an Internet-based business to provide a wide range of products at a competitive price and to supply the products to customers globally. The next chapter will discuss the importance of partnerships and how organizations maintain these partnerships with suppliers and other important parties.

CASE STUDY

Google Delights Customers With Technology Enabled Products, The Google Mobile

Want to know flight updates, sports results, stock quotes, weather reports or search for images without logging on to the net or using your laptop? Then Google Mobile is the answer where you get all of this information and more – right on your mobile, at your fingertips.

Google Mobile helps you to search your favorite restaurants serving regional cuisines, locate dry cleaners near your home, suggest businesses in your area, remembers where you are – and all these much faster and easier because then you can use your cell phone instead of your PC. And wait, it's not only these listings but more to come as you read further. You can personalize your mobile homepage, add feeds of other website, and keep tabs on the most important information. All while you are on the move and with pages of each appropriately formatted to fit your mobile's screen size. And in case you have a smart phone, you have the option to side-load and synchronizing it with your PC.

The Google Mobile is not just restricted to ordinary and routine search; you also have other features on your device that are very useful.

1. **Google Maps:** Your web-enabled mobile phone (including Java), Windows Mobile, Palm or Nokia/ Symbian devices can help you know exactly where you are, where the nearest Café Coffee Day is located, where you can get a late night buffet dinner or a last-minute bouquet for your loved one. You are alerted about the traffic jams to help you avoid taking these routes, along with detailed guidance once the place of destination is typed in.

2. **G-Mail:** Now you can send and receive messages on your handset with a new version of G-Mail that is faster using less data. Don't restrict yourself to opening just word or pdf documents because you can enjoy multimedia files like music, videos, and photos too.

3. **Picasa:** Your mobile can now store your photo albums and can be viewed anytime with the help of Google Picasa. Additionally, you have access to your friends' latest snapshots, exploring community photos and/or retrieve any of the millions of photos posted online through a built-in search facility.

4. **YouTube:** You can watch any movie, video clipping, on any subject that is of your interest, from across the world right on your hand held device. YouTube gives you access to not only the world of entertainment but to the world of knowledge.

5. **GOOG-411:** A new information service under Google Mobile, where you can search for local businesses by their name or category and connect with them directly or get more details about them through Short Message Service (SMS). All this without typing a single word because GOOG-411 understands your voice.

6. **Calendar:** Google Calendar helps you to view your schedule on your mobile unity from anywhere. You can add new events or edit the existing ones. When the mobile is synchronized with your PC, any changes done on the PC will be reflected immediately on the Google Calendar for mobile devices.

7. **News:** Keeping current with latest news at all times was never so easy with Google News, where you can search for the latest news on any topic from multiple sources worldwide. You have the option to even set-up a personalized news page as per your personal interests.

8. **Short Message Service:** SMS is a communications protocol allowing the interchange of short text messages

between mobile telephone devices. To get quick results and save you time, Google SMS comes in handy where your most frequently searched locations get saved and it is ready to answer your future queries.

9. **Blogger:** Now you can create a blog automatically by sending a message from your mobile phone, post photos to the web blog or share your experiences with others.

10. **Reader:** With Google Reader on your phone, you can get your favorite blogs and news feeds on your mobile device that can be read anywhere. Any interesting item(s) can be added to the shared information and you have the option to highlight it for access at a later time. With the synchronization option, you have the benefit of seeing news items everywhere at the same time and any items read on one device are marked as read on all.

11. **Google Docs:** Google Docs help you to access and view your documents on your mobile device. Documents are securely stored online and are adapted for viewing on a phone without additional work from you.

12. **Sync:** With the Sync option, your Blackberry calendar can be synchronized with your Google calendar while on the move. You will be delighted to receive alerts for upcoming events and appointments with sound or vibration alerts even when there is no network

coverage.

13. Notebook: With Google Notebook, you can add, edit or view notes from anywhere on your mobile device.

Providing the above features at one's fingertips, Google has not just made the life of today's busy executives and managers simpler, but it has indirectly provided more opportunities for customers. Additionally, Google has created new opportunities in the marketplace. Clients have greater access to the Internet and can do more sophisticated things at greater convenience. This is a win-win situation for all parties involved.

CHAPTER SUMMARY

You now know the meaning of a Product and that products have a classification. Items offered by businesses are categorized as either a Product or a Service. There are different levels of a product that satisfy customers' needs and preferences.

There are different stages in the development of a new product: Idea Generation, Idea Screening, Concept Development and Testing, Concept Testing, Marketing Strategy Development, Business Analysis, Product Development and Test Marketing, and Commercialization. New products are best managed through strategic audits and marketing strategies with significant consideration in segmentation and positioning.

The Product Life Cycle has four stages: Introduction, Growth, Maturity, and Decline. Various strategies can be adopted during each of the stages of a product's life cycle. There are different Product

Decisions, Product Line Decisions and Product Mix decisions that a manager must make for a successful online marketing campaign. It is important to integrate Information Technology while marketing any product.

Finally, the case study on Google covered all of the concepts related to product to provide a better understanding on this chapter. Chapter 4 focuses on how Partnerships fit well into this mix.

REVIEW QUESTIONS

1. What are the different levels of a product? Are there any important levels of them all and why?
2. What are the different stages of New Product Development?
3. What are the strategies to Manage New Product?
4. What are the strategies in the different stages of the Product Life Cycle?
5. What are the various Product, Product Line, and Product Mix Decisions?

CHAPTER 4

PARTNERSHIP

Chapter Contents

- Objectives
- Introduction
- Goals of Partnership
- Types of Partnership

  1. Forward Alliance

     1.1 Licensing

     1.2 Franchising

     1.3 Royalty

  2. Backward Alliance

     2.1 Joint Venture

     2.2 Strategic Alliance

     2.3 Contract Manufacturing

- Stages of Partnership Formation
- Causes of Partnership Failures
- Case Study
- Chapter Summary
- Review Questions
- References

OBJECTIVES

The objective of this chapter is to give a basic introduction to partnerships. Partnerships are strategic alliances that are required for sustaining competitiveness in the marketplace. The organizations involved in these alliances remain independent but assist each other by providing products, services, additional distribution options, and greater manufacturing capacity. Once the partnership is formed, the partners share the risks, revenues, and benefits of the e-business. The goal of a partnership is to access a larger share of the target market segment, provide new product offerings, and increase access to different geographic markets. This chapter illustrates how e-marketing makes these partnership goals possible.

There are two types of e-partnerships: 1) Forward Alliances and Backward Alliances. Strategic alliances involving the Internet are now referred to as e-alliances. They are the most common form of alliances in the virtual business world. This chapter illustrates the three stages of partnership formation: the initial stage, the intensive stage, and the dissolution stage. This chapter also discusses why organizations enter into partnerships, and the success and importance of partnerships with the case study on IBM.

INTRODUCTION

For businesses to perform well in the highly competitive environment of e-commerce, businesses must frequently update and maintain a wide range of product offerings. In the previous chapter, we discussed the importance of products and how businesses categorize these products. To meet the demand of the customers, the organizations enter into partnerships to supply different types of products. These products must be supplied to customers at the affordable prices and delivered to them as quickly as possible. The formation of partnerships helps businesses accomplish these goals.

Partnership refers to the strategic alliances that are required for the seller to enhance its competitiveness to succeed in the Internet marketplace. The partnership between two businesses cooperating through the Internet is termed as **E-Partnership**. An e-partnership is similar to a standard partnership, except the partnership takes place only over the Internet. These partnerships are formed either domestically or internationally so that the businesses can offer higher levels of services and form better relationships with their target consumers. One example of a successful partnership is American Online and Sun Microsystems joining together to launch Sun-Netscape Alliance iPlanet e-commerce solutions. This e-partnership has resulted in an offering of an easy-to-use comprehensive e-commerce solution. Additionally, the e-partnership has provided the broadest portfolio of Internet infrastructure and e-commerce applications software and services[32].

Partnerships are formed between two or more organizations to accomplish a set of goals previously agreed upon to meet business requirements. The incentive for forming a partnership is for both sides to increase profits and widen their customer base. In recent years, partnerships have also been advantageous to strategic business activities such as research and development. When a partnership is successful, businesses experience an increase in technological development and production efficiency. All risks, resources, benefits, and revenues are shared under the terms of the partnership.

---

32   Sun Microsystems 2000.

In 2002, a survey study of 250 companies in the United Kingdom showed that approximately 160 large companies have established e-partnerships. Today, it is very common to see online businesses maintaining a portfolio of more than 20 partnerships. Online companies, through the partnerships they form and generate 20-50 percent of their respective corporate revenue. Small and medium sized organizations have increased the value of their brand name recognition by forming partnerships with global organizations, as evidenced in the information and technology service sector. These partnerships are effective because their clients feel more comfortable if a small software development company has certified partners in its portfolio. The value of a software development company increases if a company is a Microsoft/SAP/CISCO certified partner. Online businesses can use e-partnerships to advance themselves in the competitive and dynamic e-business marketplace.

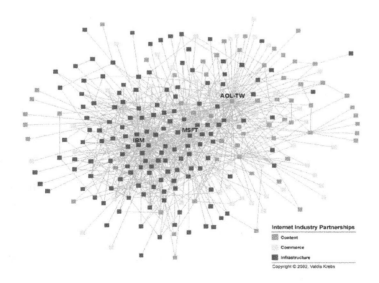

Figure 1: Internet Industry Partnership

Figure 1 represents the different partnerships of IBM, Microsoft, and America Online. The different color nodes represent different companies and the gray lines joining these nodes represent the partnerships. As can be seen from the diagram, a company can have one or many partners. The partners can be small and medium enterprises or a large organization situated in a different geographical region. A well connected organization aligns with a multitude of partners and acts in response to market conditions prior to its competitors, and can ultimately influence the market through the relationships that it forms.

GOAL OF PARTNERSHIPS

Partnerships aim to provide a wide range of products, promote innovation of new products, and achieve a competitive edge in the market. The **Goals of a Partnership** are:

- Setting new global standards
- Overcoming barriers to competition
- Increasing access to the target market
- Increasing access to new technology
- Offering a new product range
- Increasing access to different geographic markets

An example of an effective partnership is the alliance of Motorola and In-Focus[33]. This partnership's goals are to maximize profits in the market for high-performance video display panels. Motorola spent around $20 million on In-Focus and formed an equally owned joint venture. The integrated circuits of Motorola are used with the In-Focus's technology to build display panels. Through this partnership, In-Focus has benefited from the international distribution manufacturing

33   In-Focus Systems have developed a new technology that enables them to have passive matrix displays at a low cost. The url is www.infocus.com

capabilities of Motorola. In addition, this partnership has enabled In-Focus to access the huge customer database of Motorola. Motorola also benefited -- they were able to gain access to a new and specialized technology that they were unable to develop internally. The partnership also helped them to beat Japanese competitors and retain customers worldwide for the integrated chips.

A partnership also enables businesses to enter the vertical market. Accenture[34] entered a partnership with Novistar[35] to maintain its leadership in the service sector. It enabled Accenture to provide complete solutions and services, from planning to accounting to the United States petroleum industry. Novistar, on the other hand, was situated to gain by improving its position as a provider of Internet-based delivery solutions at a low cost to the energy and petroleum industry.

Another good example of an e-partnership is the partnership between IBM and BellSouth. BellSouth provides IBM with its Atlanta and Miami data centers and its connectivity. IBM services the customers of BellSouth, providing its own new customers with software services. This e-partnership has made it possible for IBM to get BellSouth's customers without a fight. On the other hand, BellSouth has gained the advantage of having specialized skills in e-business hosting services.

---

34 Accenture is a $10 billion global management and technology consulting organization. The firm has more than 70.000 people spread across 46 countries and caters to the needs of specialized capabilities and solutions across different industry segment. http://www.accenture.com/home.asp.

35 www.novistar.com. Novistar is a provider for Intelligent Process solutions. It focuses on accounting and operations software for energy industry.

CHAPTER 4

TYPES OF PARTNERSHIPS

E-Partnerships exist in two forms: 1) Forward Alliances and 2) Backward Alliances. These partnerships are made either in the form of business partnerships or technology partnerships. Technology partnerships are formed to enhance technological capabilities, as they provide hosting services, design, and website functioning for the e-business. Business partnerships are formed to create a new business or improve the existing business. The purpose is to enhance the product offering and provide a wide range of products.

1. FORWARD ALLIANCE

A **Forward Alliance** is an alliance with sellers for promotional activity, collaborative activity, product distribution, and marketing activity. These alliances or partnerships are formed to provide a more precise product range, improve the brand value of the product, increase online sales volume and provide better services. The seller provides a channel or space on their website to promote their partner's products and services. The seller also hosts the website link, so that the partners can ensure the security of their products and services through contractual agreement and fees.

The ten year alliance between Amazon.com and Toys'R'Us is an example of a forward alliance. With this partnership, Amazon.com provides a channel for the products of Toys'R'Us on its website. Customers can view the website of Toys'R'Us through Amazon.com website. Therefore, Toys'R'Us's customers can compare products and prices with other toy companies simply by visiting Amazon.com. Through this e-partnership, Amazon.com increases the product range it offers to customers, while its partner Toys'R'Us, enjoyed the benefit of accessing Amazon.com's worldwide customer base.

Another example of this type of alliance is the tie-up of Yahoo and eBay. Here, the partnership between the two enables eBay to improve its search capabilities and increase advertising graphically. Yahoo has a sole responsibility of providing graphic ads and text ads on eBay. Yahoo also gets exclusive rights to PayPal services enabling Yahoo's customers to pay for their Yahoo services through PayPal. PayPal service is also integrated into the product offerings for Yahoo merchants and publishers.

The different forms of this type of partnership are licensing, franchising, and royalties. Forward alliances in e-business are also known as e-channels or the e-marketplace.

1.1. Licensing

A **License** is a formal agreement between two parties where the licensor gives something of value to the licensee in exchange for certain undertakings. Licensing covers inventions, new technologies, software, manufacturing systems and processes, literary materials, and innovative products. It also covers a company's most valuable resource, which is Intellectual Property. This type of partnership can be long-term or short-term, but generally the most beneficial license agreements are long-term partnerships.

An example of a licensing partnership is the multi-level partnership of PayPal and other organizations. PayPal is an online e-commerce provider. Their services are used by small businesses and online merchants. The services provided by PayPal enabled its partners to accept and collect credit card payments online, accept online donations, and online merchant shopping cart. PayPal has a contractual agreement with their partners. The contract highlights the usage of its payment services and any other related products. The partners submit confidential information to PayPal and this agreement legally binds both PayPal and their partners. PayPal charges a 1.9% to 3.4% of each transaction as a fee to their partners. Additional fees associated with these agreements are set-up fees, monthly bank fees, and fraud protection fees, which are covered by PayPal for their partners.

1.2. Franchising

Franchising is a form of licensing that markets products and knowledge together for an initial fee and yearly maintenance charge. In e-businesses, an organization must ensure that the franchisee maintains the consistency of the products, service delivery, marketing, and above all, the brand image. Most online franchises are found on auction sites, e-commerce sites like Amazon.com, and retail websites like Wal-Mart. These franchises make it possible for customers to purchase their favorite brands online. These franchises require some warehouse spaces to store the products that are offered for sale on the Internet.

Wild Bird and IHOP are good examples of a franchising partnership. Wild Bird,[36] with over 300 retail outlets, is the largest franchise system that supplies bird feed to retail stores. They offer a basic and standardized e-commerce website to their e-partners to update their inventory control, distribution, and product supply. Customer use this website to find nearest retail stores that sell the desired products. In the same vein, IHOP, although a traditional brick and mortar company, has automated its management of routine business processes for all of its franchises in the area. Through the Internet, IHOP is able to effectively respond to the needs of its franchisees (partners) with respect to inventory, distribution, as well as changes in their menus, prices, and

36 www.wbu.com

products. The partners display the IHOP menu on their website so that customers are able to see all of what IHOP offers without having to leave home.

1.3. Royalty

Royalty, according to www.dictionary.com, is defined as:

a. The granting of a right by a monarch to a corporation or an individual to exploit specified natural resources.

b. The payment for such a right.

c. A share paid to a writer or composer out of the proceeds resulting from the sale or performance of his or her work.

d. A share in the proceeds paid to an inventor or a proprietor for the right to use his or her invention or services.

An organization sells its intellectual property to its potential partners to manufacture, as they are unable to fund the production due to lack of funds, commitment, time and resources. The production of computer microchips is an example of this type of partnership.

2. BACKWARD ALLIANCE

A **Backward Alliance** is defined as an alliance maintained by the sellers to reduce transaction costs and operational costs. Generally, this type of alliance is termed an e-alliance. A good example of a backward alliance is the alliance between Amazon.com and FedEx. Amazon.com and FedEx teamed up to deliver 250,000 copies of "Harry Potter and the Goblet of Fire" to Amazon's customers on Saturday, July 8, 2006. This alliance helped Amazon.com to provide speedy delivery of the book listed for sale on their website through FedEx deliveries. The alliance between a worldwide shipping company like FedEx and any retailer expands the customer base, market share, and profits of both sides. However, the effectiveness of backward alliances is not limited to the shipper/retailer relationship; contract manufacturing companies are another good example of who can benefit from backward alliances as well.

2.1. Joint Venture

A **Joint Venture** is an agreement joining together two or more parties for the purpose of executing a particular business undertaking, where all parties agree to share the profits and losses of the enterprise. Joint ventures allow the two parties to assist each other in long-term commitment of services, resources, technology and funds for a mutual benefit to all. Aspects of assisting each other include manufacturing products, providing financial aid, developing new technology, contributing specialized expertise, and establishing a presence in the targeted market that could only be reached through the joint venture. A Joint Venture becomes necessary for some businesses when there are barriers to entry in place in the target market. Joint Ventures involve significant financial and time commitments from all parties involved. It is crucial for joint ventures to encourage equal participation from each partner.

Joint Ventures create better returns through equity participation and a greater control over marketing and production. Like all businesses, partners of a joint venture face a certain degree of shared risks. Both parties associated with a joint venture enjoy a superior market presence. This superior market presence creates more customer feedback, allowing the joint venture to respond more effectively to changes in the marketplace. By combining the strengths of both organizations, the joint venture strengthens itself against its competitors. Joint ventures can also be effective internationally, as it can overcome barriers to entry and trade restrictions to create an overall better investment environment. However, joint ventures can be risky because they require a great deal of capital investment and profits may not come immediately. E-Partnerships between businesses located in different countries must also be aware of cultural differences and ensure that they can communicate effectively with one another.

General Motors, Fuji Heavy Industries, Suzuki Motors Corp., and Isuzu Motors Ltd. are joined in a joint venture. 60.2 percent of the partnership is owned by GM, and the remaining 39.8 percent of the partnership is distributed equally among the other partners. This joint venture has created an online automotive shopping service called BuyPower Japan, which made it possible for customers to shop for cars manufactured by GM, Suzuki, Subaru, and Isuzu. On this website, customers can search, select, and configure a vehicle, in addition to requesting and comparing prices for any car.

2.2. Strategic Alliance

A **Strategic Alliance** is defined as a long-term arrangement at the strategic level between organizations to improve their competitive position and performance by sharing resources and risks. The alliances formed are long term and the risks involved are mitigated in the business. It is the most common form of partnership that exists in the virtual world. Strategic alliances are different from conventional alliances.

An alliance is considered to be strategic if it meets any one of the following criteria:

- Is the prospective partner critical to the achievement of the business goals and objectives?

- Does the prospective partner have specialized knowledge and competence that will help obtain a competitive advantage?

- Will the partnership help reduce or block a competitive threat to success?

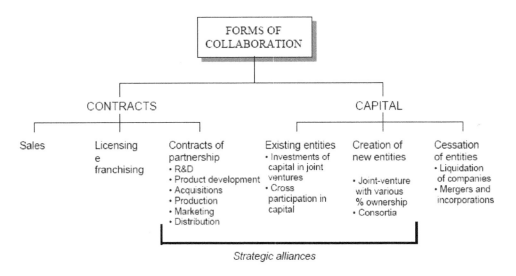

Figure 2: Strategic alliances (Forms of Collaboration)

Source: Mockler R.J. (1999), Multinational Strategic Alliances, Wiley

Strategic alliances are contracts of partnership (Figure 2), investments for existing entities, and investments in the form of capital for creation of new entities. This form of alliance can be combined with other forms of partnerships, such as franchises or licensing. The primary objective of a strategic alliance is to gain competitive advantage. A small company will benefit more if it is strategically associated with a large company with big manufacturing capacity, a wide customer base, and efficient distribution processes.

Strategic alliances are loosely structured, no-equity relationships where each partner retains its business independence. The size of the partnership is not a significant factor. Wal-Mart has strategic alliances with many small organizations with different levels of competence, thus enabling Wal-Mart to offer a wide range of products. Strategic alliances are generally established between organizations with distinctive core strengths, for example, the alliance of Amazon.com and FedEx. The core strength of FedEx is their distribution channels across the world. In the strategic alliance with Amazon, FedEx retains its independence, continuing to conduct business with other customers not associated with Amazon.com.

There are many risks involved in strategic alliances because they require significant commitments of money, time, and human capital. In the event that the alliance is terminated, the two parties must resolve issues of shared information, cost, ownership of jointly developed products, and ownership of market intelligence. The formation of strategic alliances is difficult in identification of compatible partners. In the case of an alliance between a small and big organization, there is a likely risk that the small company will ultimately be taken over by the larger partner.

2.3. Contract Manufacturing

Contract Manufacturing is a type of e-partnership in which the whole or part of a product is made by another organization, or outsourced, under a contractual arrangement. The relationship exists between the suppliers of the products and the organization. The suppliers or partners are given the desired product specifications by the organization electronically. This form of partnership reduces the manufacturing costs for the organization. However, the sales and marketing of the product is the responsibility of the main organization.

A good example of an outsourcing company is E-Business International Inc. (EBI). E-Business International Inc. provides logistics and supply chain management services between customers and suppliers. Established in 1999, the business started in Portland, Oregon. Upon expansion in 2001, the company opened an office in Chennai, India. Their contract manufacturing group consists of manufacturers situated in low cost regions of China. Therefore, EBI oversees the manufacturing of components according to the specifications from the clients. This partnership has resulted in reducing the manufacturing and production costs for EBI's clients.

STAGES OF PARTNERSHIP FORMATION

Partnership formation involves many steps and can take a long period of time. Partnership formation begins with the Initial Phase, which consists of the Strategic Planning Stage. The next step to partnership formation is the Intensive Phase, which involves the Negotiation Stage, Commitment Stage, and the Execution Stage. The final phase is the Dissolution Phase, which consists primarily of the Termination Stage (Figure 3).

When a company decides to form a partnership, it first develops a strategy in which it identifies the feasibility, objectives, and rationale of entering into the partnership. This stage is the **Strategic Planning Stage**. In the Strategic Planning Stage, the business identifies overall resources that the alliance can bring, with respect to technology, human capital, production, and business strategies. It is very important for the business to have specific objectives for entering into the alliance.

The corporate strategy should address:

- The long-term and short-term goals of the partnership
- Potential market segments for the alliance
- Availability of skills, resources, and other assets needed to achieve the alliance goals
- Core competencies of the organization
- Forecast on the overall market position of the company created by the alliance and possible competitors in 3-4 years time.

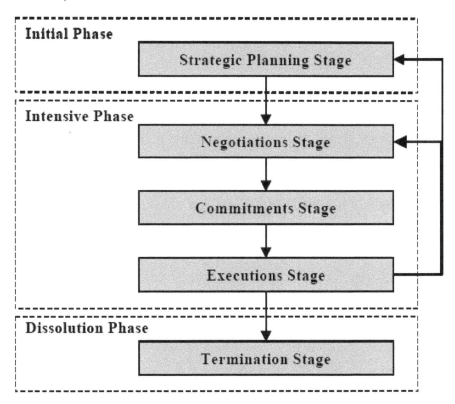

Figure 3: The Different levels of the Intensive Phase
Source: Kaasalainen, T; Makinen, S; Nasi, Juhi (2002); Looking for Company Small IT-Organizations and Partnership Formation; Frontiers of e-business research

Once the objectives of the alliance are established, the organization now moves to the intensive phase of partnership formation. There are three stages within this phase: the negotiation stage, the commitment stage, and the execution stage. In the **Negotiation Stage**, the organization assesses potential partners and analyzes their strengths and weaknesses. **Partner Assessment** involves preparation of criteria for partner selection, including understanding of potential partners' motives for entering into an alliance. One of the most important steps in partner assessment is to study the overall capacity of the potential partners with respect to resources. The organization should have a clear idea of the resource capability disparity between itself and potential partner, and should be prepared to address any gaps. All potential partners need to find ways to anticipate and fill the gaps.

Once it is decided which parties will be part of the partnership, contractual agreements are drawn up. In contract negotiation, realistic objectives of all parties are determined. The contract negotiation stage addresses contributions, rewards, and termination options for each partner. In addition, protection of proprietary information and penalties for insufficient performance are also covered in the agreement. The **Commitment Stage** involves the agreement of commitment of senior management from each side of the partnership with respect to time, budget, and resources that will be contributed to the alliance. In addition, resources are identified that helps in the transition into the partnership and the implementation of the partnership objectives, including methods for evaluating and rewarding the performance of each partner. The **Execution Stage** involves the completion of all items agreed to by the partners.

The last stage is the **Dissolution Stage**. This stage occurs when the term of the agreement is completed or if either partner wants to terminate the relationship. Criteria for premature termination of the partnership is generally outlined during the negotiation stage, when the parties agree to form the initial contract. The partners can renew the contract depending on past performance.

CAUSES OF PARTNERSHIP FAILURE

Partnerships are designed to be mutually beneficial relationships. However, the success of these alliances depends on how well the partners perform with respect to marketing and product development. Not all e-partnerships are successful, often failing due to the lack of e-management skills and viable business models. Failure can also occur due to miscommunication between parties with respect expectations and trust. However, the main cause of partnership failure is over-ambitious or unclear goals, ambiguous directions, and uncoordinated activities.

It is very important that the prospective partners understand each other's business models before venturing into the partnership. Furthermore, the business partners must be clear about the type of products and value-added services that the partnership will provide. For example, the partnership of small companies with CorProcure[37] failed because they were unable to understand the expectations of CorProcure. The management team of CorProcure failed to understand the smaller companies' specific expertise and unrealistically wanted them to enter into new areas in which these companies had no expertise.

---

37 CorProcure provided an online horizontal trading place. It facilitated aggregated auctions where smaller companies can participate in it.

The failure of furniture.com's partnership was due to lack of understanding of their logistics and distribution partners. On the other hand, its logistics partners failed to understand the importance of providing value added services. They did not perform their services quickly and efficiently, therefore causing furniture.com to be unable to fulfill customers' orders in a timely fashion.

Partnerships are formed to enter new market segments, provide a wide range of products, lower manufacturing and production costs, and improve productivity and efficiency of the organization. Productivity is vital in measuring the success of an e-business. The next chapter will define productivity and how it is measured by an e-business.

CASE STUDY

IBM, also known as Big Blue, is located in Armonk, New York. The company was started in 1897. It was a pioneer in computer hardware products. Now, it develops and manufactures services that address the needs of the information technology industry. The services include computer systems, software, networking systems, business process services, application outsourcing services, and Information Technology (IT) infrastructure. IBM offers its services to various industries like automotive, chemical, finance, and the healthcare industries. It has grouped its various services into five segments: Global Services, Hardware, Software, Global Financing, and Enterprise Investment. IBM has different development centers across the world and has set up research labs in both Europe and the Asian Pacific.

The strong revenue growth of IBM is attributed to a series of partnerships with telecom services (e.g. Bellsouth), software services (Nortel), and consultants. IBM was involved in building up the partnership from the period of 1991-92, where it engaged in 55 alliances. Forty-two partnerships were joint development in research and development and/or technological partnerships. Nine partnerships were joint ventures and two partnerships were cross-licensing agreements. These partnerships were entered in the fields of computer manufacturing and software development. The focus was more on improving the services related to operating systems, software architecture and microprocessors. Towards these objectives, IBM formed two important partnerships with Microsoft and Intel. IBM developed an agreement with Microsoft for the Windows operating system. The partnership with Intel was a long-term licensing agreement covering the development of microprocessors. These partnerships allowed IBM to develop a new product -- Wintel personal computers. IBM further entered into software development agreements with airline-companies like American Airlines. Ten strategic alliances were formed with Apple Computers to strengthen IBM's position in the domain of microprocessors and software architecture. These two companies have a non-equity research and development agreement to explore new and innovative capabilities, thus keeping the growth of their potential marketplace in view.

By 1997, IBM had increased its partnerships by entering into agreements with thirty-two more companies. It was involved in twenty-seven joint development agreements, two joint ventures, and two licensing agreements. In the past, the partnerships formed by IBM were more of a bilateral nature. However, by 1997, the collaboration between the partners became more complex and involved multiple parties. The partnerships with Toshiba and Motorola, in the field of microchips, were one of a few examples of a multiple partnership. These partnerships strengthened the existing capabilities of IBM.

IBM entered new domains like the development of multimedia and browser softwares through strategic alliances. The Big Blue also entered into a joint venture with Netscape, Oracle, Sony, Nintendo, Sega Enterprise, and NEC to develop IBM's capabilities in Internet related products and services. Through these partnerships, IBM was able to enter new markets on the Internet, including e-business solutions. IBM's careful partnership choices allowed them to establish a strong market position in providing e-business solutions by 2000. A partnership with Televerket, electronic data interchange and business consultants, enabled IBM to shift its focus from being a hardware manufacturer to a global service provider.

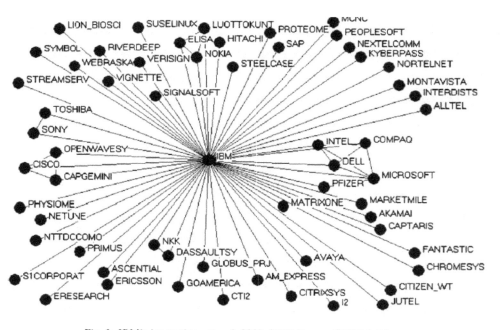

Fig. 3. IBM's innovation network 2001–2002. *Source*. CGCP database.

During the period of 2001-2002, IBM strengthened its position as a global service provider by entering into partnerships with Microsoft,

Peoplesoft, and Citrix systems. To strengthen its presence in the telecommunications industry, IBM formed a partnership with Cisco and Nortel networks. Furthermore, IBM entered into a partnership with phone manufacturers like Ericsson and Nokia. This enabled them to enter different geographic regions and maintain strong alliances with the telecommunications giants in North America, Europe and Asia.

CHAPTER SUMMARY

Partnership refers to the strategic alliances that are required for the seller to enhance its competitiveness in the global Internet marketplace. The organizations involved in these alliances remain independent, but assist each other by providing products, services, and other value-adding features to their respective businesses. Once the partnership is formed, the risks, revenues, and benefits involved in e-businesses are shared amongst the members of the organization. The primary goals of a partnership is to access a larger share of the target market segment; enter different vertical markets, offer new product ranges, and expand business to different geographic markets.

There are two types of e-Partnerships: 1) Forward Alliances and Backward Alliances. Forward Alliances are formed through licensing, franchises, and royalties agreements. They provide channels and new marketplaces for the partners. Backward Alliances are achieved through strategic alliances, joint ventures, and contract manufacturing. Strategic alliances, also called e-alliances, are the most common form of alliances in e-business.

There are three stages of partnership formation: the initial stage, the intensive phase, and the dissolution phase. The initial stage involves strategy formation and partner identification. The intensive phase involves the negotiation stage, commitment stage, and execution stage. The final stage is the dissolution phase, which involves the termination of the partnership. The major cause for failure of most e-partnerships is the failure to understand each other's business models.

REVIEW QUESTIONS

1. What is a partnership? Explain with an example of a partnership.
2. Why is a partnership important in virtual business world?
3. What is a forward alliance? Give an example of this type of alliance.
4. Explain the different between a forward and backward alliance.
5. Give an example of this type of each alliance.
6. Explain the different type of backward alliances.
7. What is the difference between a franchise and licensing? Explain with an example.
8. What is the most common form of partnership? Give an example.
9. What is the difference between a strategic alliance and a joint venture?
10. What is contract manufacturing? Give an example to explain this partnership.
11. What are the stages of a partnership formation?
12. What are the conditions that make a partnership strategic?
13. What is the major cause for the failure of a partnership?

REFERENCES

1. Adaptavist partners; accessed on 6-4-2008; http://www.adaptavist.com/display/ADAPTAVIST/PayPal+saves+the+day!.

2. Autopart reports (September 2001); http://www.allbusiness. com/technology/technology-services/813544-1.html.

3. Cazbah, accessed on 5-4-2008; http://www.cazbah.net/store. asp?pid=7952.

4. CNET news, published on 25 May, 2006; http://www.news.com/ Yahoo,-eBay-team-up-on-e-commerce/2100-1032_3-6076708. html.

5. De Man, A. P., Stienstra, M. & Volberda, H. W. (2002). E-partnering: moving bricks and mortar online, European Management Journal, 20(4), 329-339.

6. Dittich, K; Duysters,G; Mand,P (2007). Strategic repositioning by means of alliance networks: The case of IBM; Research Policy (36)1496-1511.

7. Dyer, J. H., Kale, P., & Singh, H. (2001). How to make strategic alliances work, Sloan Management Review, 42(4), 37-43.

8. Export Michigan, accessed on 5-4-2008; http://www. exportmichigan.com/ibp_pfs_strategic_alliances_and_jvs.htm.

9. Exporter Information Tools, September 2002, Strategic Alliances and Joint Ventures.

10. Graham, D. D, "E-partnerships in today's economy", CompTIA, 2001.

11. *Gomes-Casseres, B. 1989. Joint-ventures in the face of global competition, Sloan Management Review, Spring, pp. 17-26.*

12. Internet retailer; http://www.internetretailer.com/internet/ marketing-conference/41996-amazon-fedex-fire.html.

13. *Jorde, T. & Teece, D. 1989. Competition and cooperation: Striking the right balance, California Management Review, Vol. 31, pp. 25-38.*

14. http://www.corporate-partnering.com/info/strategic-alliances-partnering-examples.htm.

15. *Lei, D. & Slocum, J. 1992. Global strategy, competence building and strategic alliances, California Management Review, Vol. 35, pp. 81-97.*

16. Kaasalainen, T; Makinen, S; Nasi, Juhi (2002); Looking for Company Small IT-Organizations and Partnership Formation; Frontiers of e-business research.

17. Khanna, T., Gulati, R., Nohria, N., 1998. The dynamics of learning alliances: competition, cooperation, and relative scope. Strategic Management Journal 19 (3), 193–210.

18. Koza, M.P., Lewin, A.Y., 1998. The co-evolution of strategic alliances. Organization Science 9 (3), 255–264.

19. Kontzer, Tony; Pancake chain adopts e-business; InformationWeek, Published on 24-5-2004; http://www.informationweek.com/news/software/enterpriseapps/showArticle.jhtml;jsessionid=OPW5YOYUEKAZWQ SNDLOSKHSCJUNN2JVN?articleID=20900150&_requestid=413275.

20. Mintzberg, H., Quinn, J. B., & Voyer, J. (1995). The strategy process. Englewood Cliffs: Prentice-Hall.

21. Mockler R.J. (1999), *Multinational Strategic Alliances,* Wiley.

22. Morgan, Elizabeth; E-business Franscise http://ezinearticles.com/?E-business-Franchises&id=410002.

23. Orgnet; accessed on 5-4-2008; http://www.orgnet.com/netindustry.html.

24. Pellicelli, Anna (2003); Strategic Alliances; EADI Workshop.

25. http://www.chinesesource.net/members/cominfor.php?uid=1.

26. Sun Microsystems (2000). Palm, Inc., Sun Microsystems and iPlanet plan to develop end-to-end enterprise wireless solution. Accessed on 5-4-2008; ww.sun.com/smi/Press/sunflash/2000-2/sunflash.20000229.2html.

CHAPTER 5

PRODUCTIVITY

Chapter Contents

- Objectives
- Introduction
- Measuring Productivity
  1. Labor
  2. Capital Productivity
- Key Performance Indicator
- Productivity and Technology
- Productivity Paradoxes
  1. Measurement of Outputs and Inputs
  2. Lags Due to Learning and Adjustment
  3. Redistribution and Dissipation of Profits
  4. Mismanagement of Information and Technology
- Case Study
- Chapter Summary
- Review Questions
- References

OBJECTIVES

The objective of this chapter is to give a basic introduction to business productivity. This includes its meaning and definitions, from the manufacturing of a given product to the distribution of the product to the target and the customers. Using the Internet to conduct business has changed the way products are manufactured and distributed to customers. Partnership helps an e-enabled firm to reduce the costs of the manufacturing and supply of products. The previous chapter discussed how partnership affects the productivity and efficiency of a firm. Efficiency is an important indicator of e-business performance and an important component of productivity. This chapter defines and discusses productivity, and how it is measured in the global business environment. In this chapter the case study on e-grocery stores illustrates how online grocers came together to discover an opening in the marketplace that could better meet the needs of its potential customers by updating and expanding the corner grocer concept.

INTRODUCTION

The economic theory of **Productivity Measurement** dates back to 1942, when it was mostly focused on measuring the productivity of manufacturing and production inputs. Today, the use of the Internet by companies to conduct business online has moved productivity measurement to the e-commerce domain. The emergence of the Internet as a means of conducting business has generally helped businesses be more productive and overall has had a positive impact on the performance of the firm. The Internet functions to reduce administrative costs and search costs. In addition, usage of the Internet has helped companies distribute information about their products in an efficient manner.

Productivity is defined as the "amount of output per unit of input"[38]. **Input** refers to the labor, equipment and capital involved in creating a product or service. **Output** refers to the products and services that are generated. The revenue of a company is a good indicator of output. Output is also measured by the level of interest shown by the customers. Conducting business via the Internet allows firms to implement entirely new business models that can create competitive advantages for the firm. Additionally productivity helps the company to determine the current level of customer satisfaction they have and, in turn, help them generate new ideas.

Table 1 shows the different ways that the productivity of a company can be improved. Increased customer service is considered one of the most important benefits. Most firms have adopted the e-commerce business model and have seen an increase in productivity and profitability. For example, Ford introduced AutoXchange, which connects part suppliers and manufacturers online. Through AutoXchange, Ford created an online marketplace for its suppliers to buy and sell products. This resulted in $8 billion of savings in the first few years. Evaluation of savings is one of the best ways to measure productivity for a company who is venturing into e-commerce.

---

38 "Measuring Productivity; Measurement of Aggregate and Industry-Level Productivity Growth."OECD manual (2002)

	EXAMPLE	PAYOFF
INNOVATION	Royal Dutch / Shell's "GameChanger" teams use the Net to generate new business ideas	New "Light Touch" oil discovery method found 30 million barrels
COLLABORATION	Ocean Spray's extranet assesses cranberry quality immediately and helps growers get better prices	Growers get higher profits; Ocean Spray cuts waste and boosts productivity
DESIGN	Honeywell uses the Net to help fashion a customized prototype of anything from a fan blade to a golf club head	Design time cut from six months to 24 hours
PURCHASING	Ford's AutoXchange creates a massive online trading bazaar for its 30,000 suppliers	Could save as much as $8 billion in first few years
MANUFACTURING	BP Amoco, using Net technology from Honeywell, can quickly identify plant inefficiencies	Yields 2% per day productivity loss in Grangemouth, Scotland, refinery
LOGISTICS	Cement maker Cemex uses a Net-based truck dispatch system to speed deliveries to customers	Cement delivered within 20 minutes, down from 3 hours
MARKETING	Weyerhaeuser uses the Net to weed out its least valuable customers at Marshfield (Wis.) door plant	Boosted the plant's return on net assets from -2% in 1994 to 27% in 1999
SERVICE	GE Power Systems lets customers use the Net to compare the performance of its turbines against other GE turbines in the market	Turbine productivity expected to rise by 1% to 2% annually

Table 1: Productivity Improvement

Source: Hannula, Mika and Lonnqvist, Antii; How the Internet Affects Productivity

Other ways to measure productivity are to evaluate profits, delivery time, cost in the maintenance of a product and handling waste. However, with respect to input costs and output, since most cost reductions for Internet businesses are intangible, it becomes difficult to evaluate the productivity of the organization.

MEASURING PRODUCTIVITY

Productivity is measured to determine the efficiency of a business. Technological change, benchmark production, business process, cost savings incurred by the organization and living standards of the target market are additional considerations. Measuring productivity (Table 2) helps a company to analyze whether its different production initiatives have yielded better and more efficient output.

Type of output measure	Type of input measure			
	Labour	Capital	Capital and labour	Capital, labour and intermediate inputs (energy, materials, services)
Gross output	Labour productivity (based on gross output)	Capital productivity (based on gross output)	Capital-labour MFP (based on gross output)	KLEMS multifactor productivity
Value added	Labour productivity (based on value added)	Capital productivity (based on value added)	Capital-labour MFP (based on value added)	-
	Single factor productivity measures		Multifactor productivity (MFP) measures	

Table 2: Productivity Measures
Source: "Measuring Productivity; Measurement of Aggregate and Industry-Level Productivity Growth."OECD manual (2002)

1. Labor

Labor is a measure of work done by human beings. It is also sometimes referred to as **human capital**, which encompasses the skills and education possessed by an employee.

Labor Productivity is defined as "the ratio of a volume measure of output to a volume measure of input"[39]. **Input** is the labor which is the human capital of the organization and is generally measured by the compensation per hour for that labor. The most common measures of input are number of hours worked, workforce jobs and number of people in employment. **Output** per worker is "average product of labor".

---

39 "Measuring Productivity; Measurement of Aggregate and Industry-Level Productivity Growth."OECD manual (2002)

The volume measure of output comes in one of two types: 1) **gross output** and 2) **gross value added product,** adjusted at constant price.

- Based on **Gross Output**: The definition of labor productivity, based on gross output, is the ratio between the total quantity of gross output and total quantity of labor input. In other words, labor productivity is measured by the total market value of all final goods and services produced at a given point of time. Labor productivity indicates the labor requirements per unit of output and is a useful instrument to measure the labor requirements in a particular industry. It also reflects how productivity is impacted by the combined influence of changes in capital and other inputs. Labor productivity based on gross output is easy to measure because it only requires price indices of gross output. However, it can be easily misinterpreted as measuring the productivity of individuals.
- Based on **Value Added**: Labor productivity based on the value added services is measured through the value of goods and services produced in a particular segment of an economy. It includes wages, interests, profit, rent and indirect taxes.

Collaborative software tools like e-mail and intranets have helped to boost worker productivity. For example, technicians in the automobile industry use these tools to access onboard diagnostic systems in cars to solve minor problems from long distances. This allows the technician to fix more cars each day. Improved labor productivity will generally lead to higher income for these technicians and more opportunities for promotions and bonuses, thus contributing to a higher standard of living.

2. Capital Productivity

Capital is defined more specifically as physical capital in terms of money actually funding the business, and is measured by the user cost of capital per unit of capital service. Capital can also mean cash or goods used to generate income. Additionally, capital includes money, property and other valuables that demonstrate the wealth of a business. Capital productivity is measured as real output per unit of capital services.

Capital Productivity indicates the productive use of the capital by adding value to the business. It reflects joint influence of various inputs, technological change, economies of scale, and capacity utilization. It is measured based on gross output or value-added concept. Similar to the concept of labor productivity, it is measured by analysis of the productivity of physical capital. The difference between **value-based capital** and **gross output productivity** measures is that value-added measures are less sensitive to substitution between intermediate inputs and capital.

E-Businesses that deliver goods physically to customers require greater capital investments in logistics and distribution services. Capital is raised through equity ownership, debt, rental of equipment, or technology. Indicators of productivity for e-commerce businesses are level of customer service, product differentiation, customizing options for customers, and overall response time.

KEY PERFORMANCE INDICATOR

The **Key Performance Indicators** (KPI) enables businesses to track certain indicators on their website in order to measure business productivity. For example, Travelocity.com, an online travel company, measures its productivity by tracking the number of trips booked. They refer to their site's "contact us forms" to evaluate the number of potential customers. Generally, KPI for e-businesses are:

- **Average pages of a website viewed per session.** The time spent on a particular website is indicative of the interest of potential customer.

- **Conversion rate: the likelihood of a visitor becoming a customer.** This measure is calculated through subscription form by the customer's action. For example, customers can buy a product, register, subscribe, or show any other affirmative form of interest in the product offered.

- **Subscriptions, active subscriber base, cancellations of the subscription through the unsubscribe form.** The number of visits per month made by the subscriber is also an important indicator on the effectiveness of a website. However, productivity is measured based on cost incurred per visitor and the revenue that is generated per day by a website.

- **Shopping carts and wish lists** provide more insight into what product segment the customer has purchased from or wishes to make purchases from. It is an important indicator of the frequency of a particular customer. In addition, the average order amount/size is an indicator of the performance of a website.

- **Blog and RSS syndication** are useful indicators that measure the intangible components like brand value and consumer loyalty. These indirectly affect the productivity of e-commerce sites, as the number of blogs entered is indicative of customer interests, awareness and participation.

PRODUCTIVITY AND TECHNOLOGY

Technology refers to a collection of techniques that are used to combine resources to produce desired results. These can include tools, machines, computer software and business processes. The direct effect of technology on productivity is the reduction of redundant processes during the production process, thereby reducing various costs related to production. For example, Duramet Corp[40], a manufacturer of powdered metal, installed an inventory management system to manage and keep track of their inventory. This system helped to increase the sales without having to increase its sales force.

The indirect effect that technology brings is the changes in workplace practices, development of networks, time-saving, and changes in the type of labor involved. At Prudential Insurance, with the introduction of 8,500 laptops to the insurance agents[41], the company was able to greatly improve the productivity. Laptops helped the agent to save time while filling out 500,000 pages of forms and data every year. The agents also did not need to have face-to-face meetings with the customers, therefore enabling them to concentrate on attracting more customers. Another example is the ATM, or automated teller machine, which has

---

40 http://www.list-corp.com/b2b_directory/Dies_Manufacturers/Duramet_Corp.html
41 www.prudential.ca

helped banks provide additional convenience to customers, who can now access their bank accounts at any time.

The technology through which e-commerce is conducted is the Internet. Specific Internet technologies that are used are in the form of software like HTML and Java. The combination of these technologies in the usage of e-commerce can increase productivity by influencing production. E-Commerce affects the business process of a company and in turn affects the output and input of the company in terms of capital and labor. It has resulted in a more effective allocation of resources, and an overall reduction in maintenance costs, inventory costs, and acquisition costs incurred in production (Figure 1). In addition, the Internet has helped businesses to communicate more effectively, reducing communication and travel costs. The link between processes has become faster and more reliable, helping companies to reach wider markets.

Organizations that are investing more in information technology are experiencing a greater increase in productivity. The effect is generally seen over a period of five years, after companies have the opportunity to adjust to the initial problems that come with the implementation of new technology. Over this period of time, the employees learn and adapt to new technologies, maximizing the efficiency of the technology and ultimately increasing productivity.

Companies invest in information technology by upgrading their employees' desktop personal computers with newer models, operating systems, and updated software.

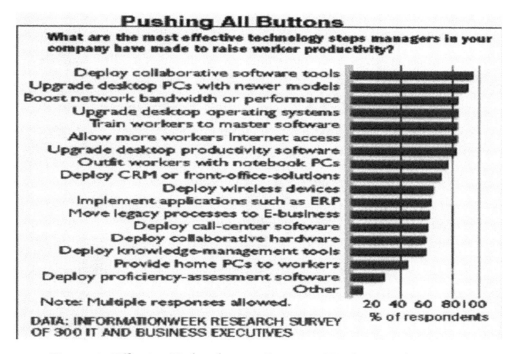

Figure 1: Effective Technology to Improve Worker Productivity
Source: McGee, Marianne K(April, 2000), "It's official: IT Adds Up" accessed on 27-4-2008;

http://www.informationweek.com/782/productivity.htm

Organizations can also make investments to improve the network bandwidth, connectivity tools, and collaborative software tools to enable workers to work from home. These expanded options have shown to increase the productivity of the workers. Currently, a higher priority is given to investing in knowledge management tools and strategic information systems. These tools are believed to have given organizations the competitive edge that they need. However, the benefits yielded by the investment in information technology have intangible and unquantifiable improvement in productivity.

CHAPTER 5

PRODUCTIVITY PARADOXES

Information has an intangible quality and its value is difficult to measure, thus creating productivity paradoxes. **Productivity paradoxes** are a phenomenon where the investments made in information technology have not yielded tangible improvement in productivity. The productivity paradoxes are categorized in four types: 1) Mismeasurement of Output and Input, 2) Lag, 3) Redistribution of Profits, and 4) Mismanagement of Information Technology.

1. Measurement of Outputs and Inputs

The low productivity of information technology is attributed to the fact that organizations now have invested significantly in information technology. These investments have yielded mostly intangible benefits, such as speed, response to customer demands, and improved customer service. This has led to a measurement problem for e-businesses, as they are unable to develop accurate, quality-adjusted price deflators. This problem is further exacerbated by the continuous introduction of new features and variations to the existing product. The convenience afforded by 24/7 ATM is considered to be an immeasurable output. Additional convenience features such as the ability to pay bills and manage personal bank accounts online are all added features that provide value to customers. These added features are the output of a fixed labor input and their productivity is difficult to measure.

Computer usage increases the quality of work life for the labor force and allows lower wages to be paid to workers because repetitive typing, tabulation, and report making are minimized with the use of computers. However, this is not to say laborers are paid a higher salary than before. In addition, inputs like software and training require huge investments, and the benefits from these investments are only observed after a few years. Even so, the investments are generally expensed on the company's financial statements the year the expenditure was made. This influences the input measurement for the company, and thus the productivity measurement becomes biased and inaccurate.

2. Lags due to Learning and Adjustment

Benefits from information technology investment take a long-time to show up on a company's balance sheet, making it difficult to determine whether productivity has improved. Time lag is a well known problem in both the economic and accounting domain. The CIO.com believes that IT investments take 5 years to payoff. In the meantime, the time taken for the employee to understand and proficiently use the technology contributes to the existence of lags.

3. Redistribution and Dissipation of Profits

The redistribution of funds to activities such as market research and forecasting adds nothing to total output. However, such redistribution help a company gain a competitive edge over its competitors through advanced knowledge of demand and supply. The introduction of strategic information systems in a company enables the company to strategically place itself in the marketplace and take profits away from their competitors. However, it is also believed that the overall profit margins for companies become smaller because the gains are distributed among consultants, IT hardware and internet connection providers.

4. Mismanagement of Information Technology

Mismanagement occurs when an organization is unable to judge whether information technology was productive at the organizational level. The obvious problem is the quantification of the benefits from IT. As the organization is unable to justify and quantify the benefits received from IT investment, the organization has difficulty making the right decisions on proper information technology investments.

There are various reasons for productivity paradoxes at the firm level. The problems measuring productivity improvement and the profitability of various business processes are a significant part of this paradox. However, new ways have been developed to overcome the productivity paradoxes and to measure productivity. This is necessary because productivity measures are indicative of customer satisfaction and efficiency.

This chapter has discussed how productivity is measured in an e-business. To attain high level of customer satisfaction, price is an important aspect. Customers' preferences are highly affected by price. Therefore, any slight changes in price will affect customer satisfaction and thus positively or negatively influence the productivity of the organization. The next chapter will discuss the concept involved in pricing a product that is sold over the Internet.

CASE STUDY

E-Grocery is a service offered where customers can order all grocery items to be delivered to their homes. Many big name stores like Safeway, Albertsons, Stop and Shop -- under the consortium of Peapod -- are members of e-Groceryusa and Supply Grocery in their respective area. These grocers are a part of e-Groceryusa and Supply Grocery throughout the USA. The website has a list of grocers sorted according to the state.

The customer can pay by credit card to purchase groceries online. Once an order is placed, there are three ways in which the groceries are supplied to the customer. The customer can have the groceries delivered to their home, collect the order from the store, or have them delivered within the delivery radius. A minimum order of $50 is required for the groceries to be delivered to home or office. The orders are distributed and stored based on the contents of the order, i.e. whether refrigeration is required or not. The most popular delivery option is home delivery, chosen by 80% of the customers. The customers are given 3 delivery slots per day to choose from. The cities where the groceries are delivered are broken down by zip code, and the grocers on that zip code supply the groceries.

Figure 2 shows the profile of online grocery shoppers. The main age group of online shoppers are customers between the ages of 29-50.

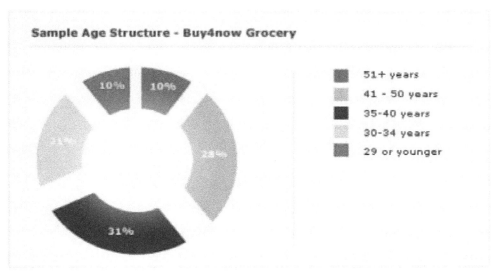

Figure 2: Profile of Online Grocery Shoppers
Source: www.e-groceryusa.com

Generally, the e-Groceryusa.com customers are those who have little time to do grocery shopping. The other segment who is actively using this website are families with children under the age of five. Their choices are influenced by wanting to make the shopping process more convenient. Busier customers who view grocery shopping to be a time-consuming task are the customers frequently using this service.

When compared to the traditional supermarket, e-grocery has shown a marked improvement on productivity. E-grocery helps customers to save time and energy in terms of fuel and money. The input in terms of labor is lower than the traditional supermarket, improving productivity across the supply chain. The value added to the customer through reduction in time and money additionally affects the output of the e-grocery and contributes to improved productivity.

CHAPTER SUMMARY

Productivity is defined as the amount of output per unit of input. Conducting business over the Internet introduces a firm to new business models. Increased productivity helps companies to improve upon existing levels of customer satisfaction, and in turn support them to generate new ideas.

Productivity is measured to determine the overall efficiency of production in an organization with respect to output and cost. Measuring productivity helps an organization to analyze whether their different initiatives have yielded a better unit of output for their products and services.

Labor is a measure of the work done by human beings. It is also sometimes referred to as human capital, which encompasses the skills and education possessed by the employee. **Labor Productivity** is defined as the ratio of a volume measure of output to a volume measure of input. **Output per worker** is "the average product of labor". Worker productivity can be increased through the use of collaborative tools.

Capital Productivity is defined as real output per unit of capital services. Improved customer services, higher levels of customization of products, more product variety, and reduced response time are considered when evaluating the productivity for organizations involved in e-commerce.

The **Key Performance Indicator** (KPI) allows the business to measure important indicators on its website that reflect its productivity and overall business success. Important indicators are: average pages of a website viewed per session, conversion rate, number of subscribers, active subscriber base, average order value/size, and Blog and RSS syndication.

Productivity Paradoxes occur where investments made in information technology have not yet yielded tangible improvement in productivity. The productivity paradoxes are categorized in four ways: 1) mismeasurement of output and input, 2) Lags due to Learning and Adjustment, 3) redistribution and dissipation of profits, and 4) mismanagement of information technology.

REVIEW QUESTIONS

1. What is Productivity? What is its importance to the organization?
2. Define labor and labor productivity? How does a firm improve labor productivity?

3. What is capital? What is capital productivity?

4. What are the components of capital productivity?

5. What is the Key Performance Indicators (KPI) for e-commerce?

6. What are the different effects of technology on productivity?

7. What are productivity paradoxes? Explain them.

REFERENCES

1. Atrostic, B. K. and S. Nguyen (2002) *'Computer networks and US manufacturing plant level productivity: New evidence from CNUS data'*, Centre For Economic Studies working paper 02-01, U.S. Bureau of the Census, Washington D.C.

2. Brynjolfsson, Erik (1993); *The Productivity Paradox of Information Technology: Review and Assessment*; Communications of the ACM; December.

3. Brynjolfsson, E. and L. Hitt (1993) *'Is information Systems spending productive*? International Conference on Information Systems.

4. Brynjolfsson, E. and L. Hitt (1996a) *'Paradox lost? Organization-level evidence on the returns to Information System Spending'. Management Science*, 42, 4, pp.541-558.

5. Brynjolfsson, E. and L. Hitt (1996b) *'Productivity, business profitability and consumer surplus: Three different measures of Information Technology value'*, *MIS Quarterly*, June, pp.121-142.

6. Jackson, Steve. *'How measuring Key Performance indicator can improve e-commerce strategy'*. Accessed on 29-3-2008. http://www.businessknowhow.com/internet/kpi1.htm.

7. Gross Value Added (GVA) Briefing Paper (pdf). Kent County Council (2007-10-29). Retrieved on 2008-03-29.

8. ECOMLOG research project's Internet site, [http://www.tai. hut.fi/ecomlog/] (Site visited May 11th 2001).

9. Hamel, G. (2001) Edison's Curse. Fortune, March 5, pp. 175-178.

10. Lewis, B. 1996. *IS Productivity Paradox Means We Should Be Measuring Effectiveness*, Infoworld, February 26, pp. 61.

11. Lucas, H. C. Jr. (1999), *Assessing the Value of Investing in IT*. New York, Oxford University Press, 225 pg.

12. OECD Manual: Measuring Productivity; www.SourceOECD. com.

13. Punakivi, M., Holmström, J. (2000) e-Grocery home delivery -a step towards Green Logistics, July.

14. Nimtez, Jody (2006); Key Performance indicators for E-Content Sites. Accessed on 29-4-2008. http://www.webpronewscanada. com/2006/0512.html.

15. McGee, Marianne K(April, 2000), "It's official: IT Adds Up" accessed on 27-4-2008; http://www.informationweek. com/782/productivity.htm.

16. Hannula, Mika and Lonnqvist, Antii; How the Internet Affects Productivity.

17. http://www.investorwords.com/3876/productivity.html

18. http://www.tut.fi/units/tuta/teta/mittaritiimi/julkaisut/internet.pdf

19. http://www.cio.com/article/31216/How_to_Measure_the_Payoff_of_E_Business_Projects

20. http://www.egroceryusa.com/dynamiccontent.aspx?loc=0

CHAPTER 6

PRICE

Chapter Contents

- Objectives
- Introduction
- Importance of Pricing and Role of Costs
- Types of Pricing
- Pricing Process
- Price Setting
- Factors Affecting Pricing
- Pricing Strategies
- Responding to Pricing Changes
- Pricing Ethics
- Case Study
- Chapter Summary
- Review Questions

OBJECTIVES

The objective of this chapter is to understand the meaning of price, the importance of pricing and the role costs play in the pricing of products and services. In addition, pricing decisions must be made while keeping in mind the perception of customers with respect to the value of the product.

This chapter illustrates the process behind how prices are set in the different segments using price metrics and segmentation fences. In addition, this chapter explores the various external and internal factors that affect the pricing of online products, and the incidental costs related to pricing. A company must follow certain pricing strategies for its new and existing products and distribution channels throughout the product's life cycle. All of these pricing decisions have rationales that are supported by the financial analysis. This chapter briefly touches on these topics to give the reader a glimpse of strategies and pricing decisions.

Companies must respond immediately to changes in market prices in order to manage and control the competition. We would appreciate as how such situations can be managed without crossing the limits of pricing ethics.

The chapter concludes with a case study that discusses how Dell uses Internet technology to sell its products directly to customers without any intermediaries, thus avoiding any price confusion. Dell's direct online selling business model gives it a competitive edge to offer products at a price far below others with a quality that is reliable. In addition, it provides its customers with the ability to customize the product they want to purchase and get it delivered to their place of choice.

INTRODUCTION

An e-business constantly monitors customer satisfaction to judge its productivity and efficiency, as was discussed in the last chapter. Due to the fact that online shoppers are very sensitive to the price of a product, price is one of the major determinants of customer satisfaction. Any slight change in the pricing of a product can result in losing that customer to another business. In this highly competitive environment, e-businesses cannot afford to lose many customers. This chapter will discuss the importance of price and the factors that affect the pricing strategy of the firm.

Price[1] is the amount of money that a customer must pay the selling party for a product or service for his consumption or use. It is a part of an exchange process[2] that involves any transaction between two parties, generally referred to as buyer and seller, where each party gives the other something in return for accepting something. At the end of the process, both parties give up something of value in return for something else of value. The customer's payment may involve a combination of money, property, and/or services.

Price should not be confused with **cost**. Price is the amount a buyer pays to purchase a product. Cost, however, encompasses more than simply price. Cost is the investment a seller makes to offer his product to the buyer. This involves labor costs, manufacturing costs, and all other incidental costs to the marketing and selling of the

1   http://www.determan.net/Michele/mprice.htm
2   http://www.knowthis.com/tutorials/principles-of-marketing/pricing-decisions/1.htm

product. Businesses must set product prices higher than the overall costs incurred in order to make profit. However, costs are not the only consideration in pricing decisions.[3] Pricing decisions are important not only for businesses trying to maximize profits, but also for non-profit organizations.

For the past century, **pricing decisions** have been dominated by three important philosophies – **cost driven**, **customer driven** and **competition driven**.

1. <u>Cost-plus pricing</u>: This pricing model is driven by the finances within the organization that penalized high volume products while subsidizing the low volume products. Cost-plus pricing is a strategy that is used to determine the price of goods and services offered for consumption. Companies of all sizes tend to use this simplistic pricing model as a guideline for arriving at sale prices that will allow the company to cover all costs associated with the production and sale of the products while still making a reasonable profit. The ultimate goal of cost-plus pricing is to allow the originator of a good or service to price goods and services in a manner that helps to ensure that all costs associated with the effort are covered.

2. <u>Customer-driven pricing</u>: This pricing model was mainly supported by people in sales. Their focus was rather misplaced, in that they looked towards the willingness of the customers to pay, rather than the value.

3. <u>Competition driven pricing</u>: This pricing model is driven mainly by marketing personnel and quite often by the engineering department. Both the marketing personnel and the engineers

---

3   www.nbuysell.com/prep-plan/market-analysis.pdf

had major problems with business objectives based on achieving a certain market share.

Each of the above philosophies have their own weaknesses in that they do not encompass all of the considerations necessary for effective pricing. Effective pricing must be value based, profit-driven and proactive. This is possible with a pricing strategy that is directed towards addressing certain questions. These include what objectives the business has in setting a price, who they expect their customers to be, and what other needs the business must meet.

IMPORTANCE OF PRICING

The marketing personnel in a business must realize that pricing[4] should be an incredibly important component of their marketing activities. When marketing products, price is the easiest variable to adjust in hopes of attracting more customers. Depending on the demand for the product, marketers can change the price instantaneously.

Pricing decisions are generally important when a business wants to increase demand for its products or react to the pricing decisions of its competitors in the marketplace. Any pricing decision must be backed by sound market analysis and research if businesses wish to maximize the returns on their products.

Pricing affects[5] the image of a company and its products. Customers' first impression of a product is largely determined by the price of the product. If a product is not selling well at its current price, the marketers must consider reducing the price as soon as possible. In addition, when

4 http://www.knowthis.com/tutorials/principles-of-marketing/pricing-decisions/3.htm
5 http://www.startmarketing.com/importance-pricing.html

a product is selling well, marketers must consider raising the price to a more optimal level that customers are still willing to pay.

Effective pricing helps to generate interest from potential customers. Hence, many sales promotion activities involve the lowering of prices to help stimulate product sales. However, it is important to note that a great deal of price fluctuation for a given product will confuse customers. The most effective pricing strategy is to reserve pricing changes for specific circumstances to keep price change as an effective method of stimulating sales and increasing returns.

According to the McKinsey Report[6], all other things equal, a 1 % increase in price creates an 8% increase in operating profits. This gain in operating profits is about double the impact a 1% decrease in variable costs has on operating profits.

ROLE OF COSTS IN PRICING

While designing the pricing strategies,[7] particularly for products targeted for the Internet, the relevant costs involved have to be thoroughly understood and identified so that companies can reliably forecast the profit impact of their pricing decisions. There are different costs involved in pricing a product that could be categorized as relevant, incremental (prices that change with volume) or avoidable. They have to be properly differentiated to keep the costs at the minimum. Exploring the accounting system and understanding the various concepts particularly relating to costs are necessary tasks for organizations to make appropriate pricing decisions. Pricing is not

6 http://www.insidecrm.com/archive/2006/04/the_importance_.html
7 Strategy and Tactics of Pricing: A guide to growing more profitably; Nagle and Hogan; Prentice Hall, 4th Edition, 2006

historical looking; it is looking forward, and calls for financial reporting to focus on total and net contribution. Hence, net profits need to be managed along with the maximization of contribution. Another way to keep costs down is transfer pricing. Transfer pricing helps the firm avoid increased fixed costs by enabling higher contribution margins, sales volume and profitability. According to Wisegeek.com[8], transfer pricing is the rates or prices that are utilized when selling goods or services between company divisions and departments, or between a parent company and a subsidiary. The transfer pricing that is set for the exchange may be the original purchase price of the goods in question, or a rate that is reduced due to internal depreciation. When used properly, transfer pricing can help to more efficiently manage profit and loss ratios within the company. Generally, transfer pricing is considered to be a relatively simple method of moving goods and services among the overall corporate family.

TYPES OF PRICING

There are various methods businesses use to price[9] their products and services. Some of the common and well known methods of pricing are –

1. **Cost Plus Pricing**: The firm charges a price that covers the total cost it incurred to produce and deliver the product to the customer, plus a certain percentage of the cost that creates profit.

2. **Break-even Pricing**: A pricing where a firm sets a price equal to its production cost. This method of pricing is only used generally by non-profit organizations.

---

8 http://www.wisegeek.com/what-is-transfer-pricing.htm
9 http://www.businessplans.org/Pricing.html

3. **Target Profit**: In this pricing, the organization clearly understands its operating costs and sets a price with the goal of making a certain percentage of profit before taxes.

4. **Perceived Value**: This method involves businesses setting the price of the product at the level they believe customers value the product.

5. **Competitive Pricing**: This method of pricing uses the competitive price level as a base for the ultimate price setting.

6. **Two Part Pricing**: This method of pricing is composed of two parts: the fixed fee, and the variable fee. This method of pricing is used most notably by utilities companies or providers of telephone service.

7. **Bundled Pricing**: This method of pricing offers several products for sale as one combined product.

8. **Psychological Pricing**: This method of pricing sets a price in a way that is psychologically more appealing to customers. For example, a producer may price a product at $49.95 instead of $50.00 to create the illusion that the product is lower-priced than it really is.

PRICING PROCESS

Businesses should establish a pricing policy that considers not only customers' perception of the value of the product, but also their expectations and the amounts that they would be willing to pay for the product. Customers perceive discounts and promotional schemes offered by businesses as a response to price competition. However, businesses can use methods such as ad-hoc pricing and special pricing to give their sales personnel more flexibility in increasing sales volume. Businesses must have sound pricing policies that can utilize different methods of pricing to achieve greater profitability.

Generally, companies that decentralize their pricing policy and delegate all pricing authority to their field executives have poor financial performance. Therefore, a centralized pricing authority, where the executives work within a given framework is an ideal situation. The **pricing policy** helps to define rules and procedures within which the employees and customers can operate. This enables the company to train its customers to get the best deal they can expect from the prices listed and what tradeoffs are available at given price levels. The sales personnel gain a set of standard tools that facilitates the sales process by giving customers more options and helping them to get the value they expected from the product to make tradeoffs on the prices listed so that they get the value they expected from the product for a price they are willing to pay.

PRICE SETTING

Companies must set the right prices for their products in the various market segments in which they participate.[10] To set the right prices, companies must maintain updated data on their customers and competitors. For pricing to be effective, it needs to be economically acceptable to both the company and the customer – i.e. value-based pricing. The effectiveness of pricing is best judged by field managers who constantly interact with prospective customers and understand their needs.

Price setting is driven by a measure called the Differential Value Capture Rate, or DVCR. DVCR is a measure that is designed to assess certain factors, such as the product's life cycle and buyer sensitivity to price changes. Another key consideration is the long-term pricing

---

10 Strategy and Tactics of Pricing: A guide to growing more profitably; Nagle and Hogan; Prentice Hall, 4th Edition, 2006

strategy of an organization. It is important for the managers to gather and calculate the value capture rate, not only for their own customers but also for their competitors.

Based on customer reaction to a given price, **price optimization** is achieved through test marketing. Price optimization is a necessary adjustment process to maximize the profits where a company will assess their costs and expected sales volume at various prices and make the best price choices. This is done by examining the strategic objectives of the organization, the kind of response customers give to the change in price, and the final price that is set. Each subsequent price adjustment helps an organization learn something important either about consumer preferences or about market conditions. These price adjustments are combined with break-even calculations to bring the organization closest to the optimal price.

Price changes can be risky, and require careful planning and strategy for effective implementation. Any customer feedback or objection to a price change must be effectively addressed by the organization's personnel, who must provide a reasonable justification for the price change to maintain customer satisfaction.

FACTORS AFFECTING PRICING

There are many factors[11] that can affect pricing. They can be divided into two categories – internal factors and external factors. The internal factors include:

- the marketing objectives
  - o return on investment

---

11 http://www.knowthis.com/tutorials/principles-of-marketing/ pricing-decisions/4.htm

- o market share
- o cash flow
- o profit maximization
- marketing strategy
- costs
  - o fixed costs
  - o variable costs

These internal factors are within the control of the organization and can be modified at any time.

The external factors include:

- elasticity of demand
  - o elastic demand
  - o inelastic demand
  - o unitary demand
- customer and channel partner expectations
- competitive and related products
  - o direct competitor pricing
  - o related product pricing
  - o primary product pricing
- government regulations

The external factors, however, are not within the control of the organization.

PRICING STRATEGIES

Effective pricing strategy is necessary for e-businesses to maximize profits. A common problem for e-businesses is that they fail to understand what online shoppers expect to pay for their product or service. Research data on Internet[12] business shows that when businesses fail to price optimally, their total revenues drop by 50% sometimes

---

12 http://www.marketingprinciples.com/articles.asp?cat=364

causing the businesses to fail. Research also shows that when people make purchases online, they expect to pay 10-20% less than they would be buying the product in person. The failures of many businesses today mainly step from lack of knowledge with respect to charging optimal prices during the different stages of a product's life cycle. Technological advances have led to the availability of software that helps managers decide what the optimal prices are to be charged to different segments in the market. At the same time, information technology has made pricing[13] more difficult in certain aspects. Generally, there are three different types of pricing strategies which are used by both online and offline marketers – fixed pricing, dynamic pricing and barter pricing.

Fixed Pricing

Under this pricing strategy, the seller fixes the price and the buyer can either accept or reject the product at that price. This model is mostly practiced by offline retailers as well as many online retailers where all types of customers are charged the same price. There are two commonly used fixed pricing strategies that Internet businesses use: leadership pricing and promotional pricing.

> **1) Leadership Pricing**: Under this model, the product is priced at the lowest possible point, and the business commands leadership position in the market because of its low pricing. This strategy is successful only when production costs are kept to a minimum while maintaining product quality on par with the remainder of the market. Leadership pricing is possible only when companies are experiencing economies of scale. However, there are many online companies who sell the

---

13   E-marketing, Judy Strauss, Adel El Ansary, Raymond Frost; Prentice Hall, 3rd Edition

products below market value and recover their losses through additional advertising revenue on their websites.

2) Promotional Pricing: This strategy is followed by online retailers who want to target first time online customers, in addition to regular online shoppers. Promotional offers are sent in bulk to prospective customers, detailing the discounts and offers that are being given. This can include simple discounts but also other discounts based on how quickly the customer responds to the promotion. For example, certain promotions are made offering lower prices if the customer buys a higher quantity or within a specific period of time.

Dynamic Pricing

Under this pricing strategy, different customers are offered products at different prices. Unlike fixed pricing, this pricing can be initiated either by the buyer or the seller. This strategy is followed to optimize overall sales and to satisfy each customer individually. The best example of this is the pricing of plane tickets, where prices are subject to change several times daily. Dynamic pricing is composed of segmented pricing, negotiation, and bartering.

1) Segmented Pricing: Products are sold at different prices depending on the segment of the marketplace.

2) Negotiation: The price of a product is negotiated between individual customers and the seller. Prices often change many times before a final price is fixed and agreed upon.

3) Bartering: Under this pricing strategy, goods and services are exchanged for other products without the usage of money. This pricing strategy has been used since the dawn of time and is not very profitable. However, those who barter will enjoy tax benefits.

PRICING STRATEGIES

Pricing objectives and strategies[14] are affected by the different stages of the **Product Life Cycle**. Therefore, appropriate pricing strategies at each stage of the Product Life Cycle helps to generate good sales and higher profits. Pricing adjustment need to be considered at the **Introduction Stage**, the **Growth Stage**, the **Maturity Stage** and the **Declining Stage.**

During the Introduction stage, the pricing objective should be to offer the product at a price that will attract consumers unfamiliar with the product. This can be done through trial promotions, direct sales, and other distribution channels. As consumers' demand increases, prices and revenue will also increase for the business. This leads to increased money available for research and development, along with the offering of new product trials and additional consumer services.

The pricing objectives in the growth stage shift from the initial attraction of consumers to product differentiation and strengthening competitive advantage. The business is trying to accomplish two goals with its pricing: offering greater product value through differentiation and still appealing to customers who are sensitive to price changes. In other words, a marketer should try to achieve a price balanced between

---

14 Strategy and Tactics of Pricing: A guide to growing more profitably; Nagle and Hogan; Prentice Hall, 4th Edition, 2006

a pure differentiated product strategy and a pure leadership strategy with respect to price.

During the maturity stage, the company's pricing objective should now stress on entering different market segments where consumer demand is more sensitive to prices. These segments generally emerge through new channels like discount stores, direct mail and Internet.

During The decline stage, pricing objectives include several pricing approaches where the marketer chooses from different options like retrenchment, harvesting or consolidation. There is more of a focus on harvesting profits from customers who are not price sensitive and are loyal to the organization. Cost are minimized, as there is a decline in sales volume throughout the market.

RESPONDING TO PRICE CHANGE

Managing competition[15] is one of the most important considerations for a marketer during the pricing decision. Reducing prices is a powerful tool that most competitors use to achieve short-term gains at the potential cost of long-term negative consequences. Pricing strategy is basically guided by game theory, and it is upon the marketer to pick the right playing field. Competitors must understand that reducing prices to gain short-term market share is a negative sum game in which all parties are subjecting themselves to potential losses. The success of a firm depends on the price charged and the response of customers[16] and competitors. Therefore, an organization must

---

15   Strategy and Tactics of Pricing: A guide to growing more profitably; Nagle and Hogan; Prentice Hall, 4th Edition, 2006
16   http://corkuniversitypress.typepad.com/cork_university_press/files/managing_price_competition.pdf

thoroughly analyze the competitive situation and respond to any price change in the market in an effective way.

Any pricing decision should be made through effective internal communications within an organization. These decisions should be made with consumer preferences and competitors' strategies in mind. A successful pricing strategy will always take into account the long-term effects a strategy will have on the level of competition in the marketplace.

Most organizations target market share instead of market segments, believing that greater market share automatically means greater profits. However, this strategy will not offer the highest quality of services to customers and businesses will be again forced to reduce prices to retain their market share. Therefore, any information marketers gain should be strategically used by focusing on increasing their own market strengths, instead of concentrating on the practices of their competitors.

PRICING ETHICS

Businesses must maintain ethical behavior during the pricing of its products to enjoy long-term benefits. However, some firms engage in unethical pricing practices for short-term gains.[17] Some unethical pricing methods used by businesses organizations are:

> **Price Fixing**[18]: Under this practice, all sellers in a market come together and conspire to fix the price of a product at a higher level and sell to consumers at this fixed price to gain more profits.

17 http://en.wikipedia.org/wiki/Marketing_ethics#Pricing_ethics
18 http://en.wikipedia.org/wiki/Price_fixing

Price Skimming[19]: Under this practice, marketers of new products will charge customers increasingly high prices to recover for their sunk costs and maximize profits prior to competitors entering the market.

Price Discrimination[20]: Under this practice, customers are charged different prices for the same product by a single provider.

Predatory Pricing[21]: Under this practice, prices are fixed at a level so low that no competitor can survive in the market, nor can any new competitor profitably enter the market. This is also termed as destroyer pricing.

Supra Competitive Pricing[22]: Under this method, the product is priced much higher than any of the competitors in the market. This generally happens in the case of such products that cannot be provided by competitors. For example, if a new drug is launched that is the only potential cure for a given disease, it will command very high prices in the initial stages of its product launch prior to market entry by competitors.

Price War[23]: Under this method, prices being lowered by one competitor induces other competitors to lower their own prices, creating a price war. These arrangements are very beneficial to consumers but ultimately hurt businesses in the market.

19 http://en.wikipedia.org/wiki/Price_skimming
20 http://en.wikipedia.org/wiki/Price_discrimination
21 http://en.wikipedia.org/wiki/Predatory_pricing
22 http://en.wikipedia.org/wiki/Supra_competitive_pricing
23 http://en.wikipedia.org/wiki/Price_war

Bid Rigging[24]: This is an illegal practice where two or more of competing bidders have an agreement in which they agree on the bid amount and allocate bids amongst each other.

Dumping[25]: This is a practice that is more prevalent in the international markets, where the products are dumped or exported to foreign countries at a price that is below the producing country's price or even below the cost of production.

Although some of the above practices are not unethical, they may be illegal depending on the governing law. It is in the best interest of an organization to avoid engaging in practices that create a long-term negative image of the organization.

This chapter has highlighted the importance of pricing and has discussed in detail the different pricing strategies used by the e-enabled firm. One of the strategies that e-enabled firms use is to outsource the manufacturing of products to companies where the production costs are lower. This is referred to as placement of product in the e-commerce environment. Place refers to the manufacturing, distribution and placement of products throughout the Internet. The next chapter will discuss the concept of place and how it is used in the virtual world.

---

24 http://en.wikipedia.org/wiki/Bid_rigging
25 http://en.wikipedia.org/wiki/Dumping_%28pricing_policy%29

CASE STUDY

DELL INC. PRICING OBJECTIVES and STRATEGY

Dell Inc, the second largest PC maker in the world, initially started its website, dell.com, in 1994 as a static page. Later entering into the world of e-commerce, it became the first company recording online sales in the millions of dollars by 1997, and for the fiscal year of 2008 its net income reached $679 million. Their website is viewed a billion times by Internet users every year, and almost half of the company's revenues are generated from its website. Dell is a premier provider of wide varieties of products[26] and services that include laptops, desktops, servers and storage system developments, software developments and documents, enterprise solutions, test engineering, displays, projectors, TVs, and printers. Dell follows the direct business model, where there are no middlemen or retail outlets. This provides its customers with superior value, technology, support and services; customizing the products and services in accordance with consumer preferences requirements and offering them a wide selection of software and peripherals that customers find easy for purchase as well as use.

Most of Dell's products are the first to enter the market, with the company having an edge over its competitors. Thousands of Dell's product development teams, along with their engineers, work hard daily to provide answers to the challenges of customer technology. This not only is beneficial for Dell, but also for its customers who are receiving high quality products at lower cost. The customers also have additional advantages of choice and control, where they themselves can assemble their computer with the software and hardware features of their choice. While 85% of their business comes from B2B, the

26 http://digitalenterprise.org/cases/dell.html

remaining is contributed by B2C. To facilitate B2B sales, they have an individualized interface for their business customers where final orders automatically come to Dell after approvals from different departments. Dell maintains its front office so well because of its efficient supply chain.

However, sales for Dell dwindled and its market share decreased in 2006. In the US market, Dell was losing ground to HP. Its revenue growth was only 6 %, as compared to HP's 10%, (even PC sales dipped from 16.9 to 16.5 % as compared to HP that increased from 13.8 to 14.9 percent). In response, Dell planned to expand itself through other routes of distribution channels. Dell set-up small kiosks in large malls and shopping centers that are a hybrid between Internet business and in-person stores. This gave customers a place to go to shop for Dell products with e-commerce options for superior customization. They also added retail partners and other value added resellers to their list globally, including Wal-Mart, BestBuy, Carrefour, and Gome Electrical Appliances Holding. They entered into an agreement with Infinity Retail in India to sell its laptops and desktops through the Chroma chain of stores. To optimize price position for online visitors, Dell offered free shipping, price discounts, free memory upgrades, free accessories, different financing arrangements, and service arrangements. These offerings furthered Dell's marketing and pricing strategies.

To improve customer support infrastructure in response to an increasing number of service complaints, Dell made an investment of $100 million to improve their customer service. With so many new changes brought to increase revenue and profitability, it remains to be seen how well off Dell will be in the future. Dell has not only maintained its direct online selling, but also entered itself into the market of using traditional methods to sell its products. However, Dell still may need new product initiatives in the future to maintain profitability and high market share.

CHAPTER SUMMARY

The chapter begins by giving the meaning of price and touching on the various pricing philosophies that have been followed for a number of decades. This chapter covered the importance of pricing and the role costs play in the pricing of the product. In addition, this chapter has covered the different types of pricing that many organizations follow. There are many factors, internal and external to the organization, that affect the setting of price.

To optimize the price and maximize returns, an organization needs to have an effective pricing strategy. We have discussed the different pricing strategies followed by both online and offline retailers. It is also important to strategically price the products at different stages of the product's life cycle to maintain sales and profits. This chapter has outlined the strategies that must be followed for each of the stages of a product's life cycle. Any change in competitors' pricing needs to be effectively responded to, and the chapter discusses how businesses should respond and manage themselves when faced with the pricing behavior of their competitors. This chapter also covers the ethical considerations involved in pricing, and how the law may also influence pricing practices.

The chapter ends with a case study on Dell, a prime example of a company that is changing its pricing strategy because of increasing competition and a market recession. The case study shows how Dell has used pricing strategies in both direct and indirect sales channels to further expand.

Try to answer the questions below after studying the chapter, using your own industry experience and classroom discussion on the case study and concepts.

REVIEW QUESTIONS

1. What is the importance of pricing and what role do costs play in the pricing strategies?
2. What factors need to be considered when businesses set prices?
3. What types of different pricing strategies can businesses use?
4. What pricing strategies have to be followed during the different stages of product life cycle?
5. How do businesses respond to a change in price by their competitors?
6. What are some examples of unethical and illegal pricing practices that are sometimes used by marketers?

CHAPTER 7

PLACE

Chapter Contents

- Objectives
- Introduction
- Supply Chain Management
- E-Commerce
    1. B2B (Business-to-Business)
    2. B2C (Business-to-Consumer)
    3. C2B (Consumer-to-Business)
    4. C2C (Consumer-to-Consumer)
- E-Procurement
- E-Collaboration
- Conclusion
- Case Study
- Chapter Summary
- Review Questions
- References

OBJECTIVES

The objective of this chapter is to give a basic introduction to place, including its meaning and definitions. This chapter introduces supply chain distributions and placement. The placement of the sellers URL (retailers and manufacturers) on the World–Wide-Web makes a difference in consumer traffic. These URL attracts customers and directly affects the consumer traffic. The case study in this chapter illustrates how consumer traffic can be increased by placing the web-link in search engines such as Google, Yahoo, and on popular websites like eBay, Amazon, and Wal-Mart. Place is an important component of the supply chain management of a seller and is generally the back end of the business.

INTRODUCTION

The Internet has changed the way the traditional supply chain is managed. The new technology afforded by the Internet has helped to reduce the cost of the product and led to lower prices to consumers. The previous chapter dealt with the importance of pricing and the different pricing strategies used by businesses. It also explained the factors that affect pricing changes. One of these factors is the environment in which the business is operated. The Internet environment has become dynamic and competitive, forcing companies to respond quickly to their competitors in order to survive. The customer expects fast and efficient delivery of products. Therefore, the organization needs to adapt its distribution and logistics placement to meet customer demands effectively. The distribution of products becomes more challenging when the demand is to supply the product to customers in different countries. The organization has to address these distribution issues through partnerships, alliances, and the use of advanced technologies like Electronic Data Interface, (EDI). This chapter deals with the concept of place and its main features.

Place refers to the placement, logistics and distributions of products throughout the internet. It also refers to the place of purchase of a product, along with the consumption of services, like games and media. The distribution of the product is an important part of marketing strategy. In the world of Internet business, the channel of distribution of the product is the manufacturer's website. The sellers' webpage is the place where the product and its specifications are placed. The way the product is presented is what will turn a potential buyer into an actual buyer. The seller can only sell products through the Internet if there are many consumers visiting their website. The seller must make a large investment of time and resources to market its website effective. The website generally is recognized as the front end of the business.

SUPPLY CHAIN MANAGEMENT

Another important aspect of place is the complex process of delivering the product from where it is produced to where the consumers demand the product. This process involves numerous suppliers, manufacturers, exporters and other distributions channels (Figure 1). These parties are all part of the Supply Chain Management (SCM) team. **SCM** is the management of the dual flow of materials, equipment, finances and information within and among the firms and its suppliers. SCM ensures efficient and fast delivery of products to the end customers. SCM has five components: **Plan** (strategy to execute the SCM program), **Source** (various suppliers), **Make** (the description of the products), **Delivery** (distribution and logistics) and **Return** (customer service). Place, in the world of Internet business, overlaps with the delivery component of the traditional supply chain management.

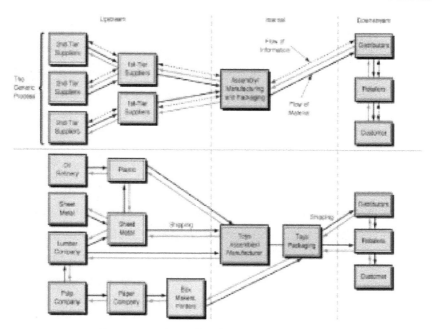

Figure 1: Supply chain management
Figure1: Supply Chain Management Process
Source: my.fit.edu/~jbarlow/BUS5460/summer2003/Chapter6.ppt

Technological advantages have blurred some of the components of traditional SCM and a new e-SCM has developed. E-SCM has changed the way business is conducted. It has helped sellers and their suppliers to deliver products quickly and effectively. In e-supply chain management, most of the processes of the traditional SCM are automated and are part of e-procurement and e-collaboration software applications. **E-Procurement** and **E-Collaboration** software help the sellers or companies to procure products from suppliers and deliver the products to the customer, respectively. The software helps companies to support data sharing both 'upstream' (to company's suppliers) and 'downstream' (to company's customers and clients).

Suppliers are able to effectively and efficiently respond to customers' needs through e-commerce, e-procurement and e-collaboration. These are the major components of place, which makes it possible for the organization to distribute and sell products to its customers (Figure 2). The seller, who is able to automate most of its SCM process into e-commerce, e-procurement and e-collaboration process is known as an e-enabled organization. An e-enabled organization has a dynamic network of customers and suppliers, because all sales and supply chain management is dealt with electronically. As products are demanded in different countries, companies must commit significant resources to be able to provide customers with its product. Companies use their e-collaboration tools to form partnerships and alliances with other organizations to supply and deliver their products to their customers. The only process that does not take place electronically is the ultimate delivery of the desired product to the customer's doorstep.

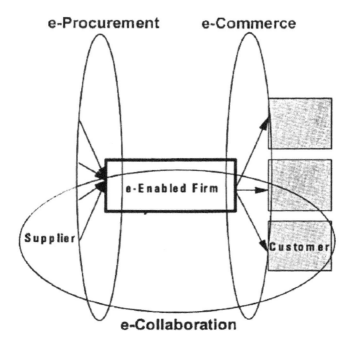

Figure 2: Components of Place

Source: Johnson, E and Whang S (2002); E-business and Supply chain
Management; an Overview and Framework; Production and operation
management; Vol 11 No.4.

E-COMMERCE

In recent years, the "bricks-and-mortar" retail channels are using the Internet as their direct channel of distribution for their products and services. **E-Commerce** refers to the exchange of goods and services electronically. The direct method of product display and information is through the company's website. All business operations, including sales, marketing, advertising and promotions are completed through computer networks such as the Internet, electronic data interchange (EDI) and/or value-added networks (VANs). The Internet is the most commonly used network through which the organization prepares a webpage to lists its products and services. The business uses online forms to collect the necessary payment information and delivery address. The Internet makes it easier for businesses to send information to their partners to better identify and respond quickly to consumer needs and preferences.

An ideal and successful e-commerce site is one which has an extensive list of products, a user-friendly interface, competitive prices, customization options for their products, and webpages fit to operate at high speeds. Web companies like Amazon and Dell are considered to be successful because they offer numerous products and provide nearly infinite customization options to their customers. Amazon.com, in addition to their huge product offering, allows customers to review and rate products they have purchased. This helps provide new customers with additional information about the product offerings and creates a very convenient shopping process. Dell offers customizable computer products for the varying needs of their consumers. Additionally, Dell provides online assistance and technical support for their customers, helping to ensure long-term customer satisfaction.

E-Commerce exists in many forms. The newer forms of e-commerce are related to government transactions, such as Government-to-Government (G2G), Government to Business (G2B), and Citizen to Government (C2G). However, this chapter will focus on the more popular and common forms of e-commerce: Business to Business (B2B), Business to Consumer (B2C), Consumer to Business (C2B) and Consumer to Consumer (C2C).

1. B2B (Business-to-Business)

B2B is the relationship between to businesses exchanging products and services through the Internet. Generally, this relationship exists between the different stakeholders of the supply chain management team. This includes manufacturers, distributors, wholesalers, and retailers. The price of the product is often negotiable between businesses, and in large part is dependent upon the quantity demanded of the product. In B2B relationships, the businesses are the customers for the other business and the end user customers shop online using the company's website. B2B websites generally fall into five categories:

I. Company Websites: Company web sites are used not only to attract more business from consumers, but also to sell their products directly to other businesses. Wal-mart.com is an example of this category of B2B website. The products are displayed on the website according to their type and distinguishing features. If the customer wishes to purchase only toys, they can sort the product type by 'toy' and check out the different toys available. The customer can also register with the website and will be informed about upcoming discounts and sales available on the website.

II. Product Supply and Procurement Exchanges: These are websites where the purchasing agent shops for supplies, including requests for certain products and maybe a bidding process. The Procurement exchange[1] is an example of this type of B2B website. It provides "one stop shopping" public procurement solutions for the public sector, thereby reducing the overall cost and time involved in procurement.

1   http://www.procurementexchange.com/ is a Canadian exchange.

III. Specialized or Vertical Industry Portals: The purpose of these websites, apart from buying and selling, is to provide information. The site provides product listings, discussion groups, and other features of a specialized area, such as Open Source Systems or industry segments like the automobile industry. These sites are particularly useful to small businesses or startup companies, as they provide useful ideas and product information. One example is, VerticalPortals.com, where lists of web portals are provided, based on a particular area of interest or information. The business can log into these websites to access the listing of businesses they are interested in.

IV. Brokering Sites: The purpose of these websites is to be an intermediary between a business who wants to lease products or services from another business, and the business that is the product or service provider. These brokering sites can charge fees for the services they provide. For example, bookmarket. com[2] is a website that lists the different print brokers or print brokering sites available. It also allows for the addition of new print companies to let site visitors to know their services are available.

V. Information Sites: The purpose of these websites is to provide information about a particular area of interest or particular industry. For example, webmd[3] provides information on various diseases, ailments, and any information related to healthcare. It is one of the most popular websites on the Internet, and people anywhere can use the website to check diagnoses and

---

2 http://www.bookmarket.com/printgp.htm
3 http://www.webmd.com/

treatment for their own ailments. The website also provides an 'Ask The Doctor' section where people can submit questions about anything related to medical care via email.

2. B2C (Business-to-Consumer)

B2C is the relationship between a business and consumer (Figure 3). Customers purchasing books from Amazon.com is an example of a B2C relationship. B2C refers to online trading and auctions, where the purpose is to entice visitors for the purpose of generating sales. Chapters.com and Macy's.com are two examples of websites where the product is purchased by a consumer from the company's website.

In B2C, the flow of information, including product details and payment information, is all through the Internet. The B2C model helps businesses communicate instantaneously with the individual. In addition, the B2C model enables businesses to reach customers in global markets. The B2C model has also given customers more ability to customize product offerings to meet their own preferences and created a greater availability of products.

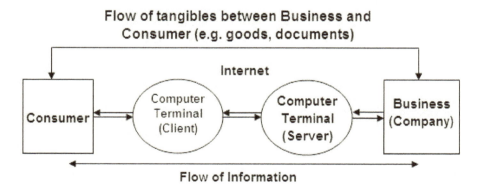

Figure 3: B2C model enabled by Internet
Source: www.crito.uci.edu

More examples of B2C websites are auction stores like eBay.com[4], online stores like Amazon.com, and online service providers like Travelocity.com[5]. On e-auction sites, bidding is done through electronic means only and can be accompanied by multimedia presentations of the goods available for purchase. In online stores, the marketing, in terms of promotion and selling of company's products, is done through the website. For online services, the company's website is used to provide customer services. Companies like www.eTrade.com have helped people to purchase and trade stocks over the internet.

3. C2B (Consumer-to-Business)

The relationship between the consumer and a business defines the term C2B. The consumer posts a set of requirements on a website and businesses review and respond to these requirements via a bidding process. It is the consumer who then selects the business based on the most effective bids. In this type of model, the items to be promoted, advertising banners and text ads, are displayed on the personal websites and the advertising company's commissions are often paid to the individuals who are hosting the ads. Online advertising sites like Google Adsense, found at www.google.com/adsense, and www.Elance.com are examples of successful C2B relationships. Google Adsense is a program that gives revenues to the web publishers for the publishing of Google advertisements on their website. www.Elance.com is another example of this type of e-commerce. It provides a meeting place for employees and employers.

---

4 eBay.com is Internet company that has online auction and shopping website where the customers and businesses buy and sell goods using the auction model of business.

5 Travelocity.com is an online travel agency where people or businesses can book tickets for air, rail and bus at a competitive price. It also has facilities to book for hotels and restaurants.

Other C2B examples are online surveys and blogs. In online surveys, the companies pay individuals to answer their survey questions. Gazingsurveys[6], Surveyscout[7] and Survey monkey[8] provide online surveys and pay individuals to participate. Blogs have become a very popular form of C2B transactions. In this model, revenues are calculated based on the consumer traffic and the individuals are paid for the number of people who have read their blog. Additionally, podcasting, video casting, and Really Simple Syndication (RSS) are all models for C2B and have provided routes for generating alternative revenues for businesses.

4. C2C (Consumer-to-Consumer)

This type of e-commerce involves transactions between individuals. There are many sites which host forums and auctions, and the consumer can use these sites to buy and sell products on their own. An example of C2C is eBay's auction service, where the products that are to be auctioned are displayed and consumers can go to the website to buy or sell any products.

E-PROCUREMENT

E-Procurement is the procurement of supplies and services over the Internet from suppliers. It is a B2B relationship between the seller and its suppliers, and is also commonly known as the supplier exchange. Once the customer orders a product, the sellers need to procure many different products from its suppliers to provide the customers their end product (Figure 4). The Internet enables the sellers to manage this process in a convenient fashion. Other value added services, such as transportation, warehousing, and custom clearing are also performed

6   gazingsurvey.com
7   http://www.surveyscout.com/main/
8   http://www.surveymonkey.com/

through the Internet. Under an e-procurement arrangement, the sites allow registered businesses to buy or sell goods and services with the buyers or sellers. The seller's site allows for customers to place bids and view prices of the suppliers' products.

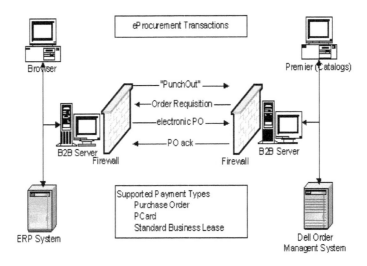

Figure 4: E-Procurement Processes

Source: www.crito.uci.edu/git/publications/pdf/dell.pdf

E-Procurement is made more effective with the use of software specially designed to automate the processes of buying and selling materials. The use of e-procurement software enables organizations to manage their inventories effectively, reduce the overhead costs for the purchasing agent, reduce operating costs, and to improve their manufacturing cycles. Companies like Ariba and CommerceOne have developed web-based procurement software that allows for real-time trading between the seller and suppliers over the Internet. This software also automates the internal procurement processes from requisition to order to payment. Procurement software can be used in many different industries and markets. Some examples of e-procurement software are the following: **Covisint**[9] is used in the automobile industry, **Exostar**[10] in the aerospace industry and **Transora**[11] in the grocery delivery industry.

The increasing number of success stories has led to many firms adopting e-procurement in their supply chain management. However, e-procurement initiatives bring about major security concerns for participating businesses. E-Procurement processes involve the movement of sensitive information over the Internet, and companies take a risk when they transmit private information over the Internet. This problem is compounded with the increasing number of cases involving data theft crimes on the Internet. Another major issue that is faced by companies using e-procurement initiative is the quality of goods. Procuring the goods through the Internet means that there is some doubt about the quality of goods, and the businesses become very dependent on the goodwill of the suppliers.

The main advantages of e-procurement are that important business processes become automated, and that e-procurement provides a

9   http://www.covisint.com/. This company was founded as consortium of the world's largest automobile manufacturer-GM, Ford Motors, DaimlerChrysler, Nissan and Renault. It is global provider of interoperability solutions and services that caters to the need of automobile industry. Currently, it has spread its wings to other areas like healthcare, and financial services.

10   http://www.exostar.com/. It is the leading provider of multiple enterprise solutions for secure information sharing, collaboration and business process integration. The company caters to the special need of aerospace and defense industry.

11   http://www.transora.com/home.html. It is community of manufacturers and Gemmar systems International and retailers. They are dedicated to developing technology solutions that helps them to lower the supply chain costs.

way for businesses to find new suppliers. There are **five** main types of e-procurement: Web-based Electronic Resource Planning, E-Maintenance Repair and Operating, E-Sourcing, E-Tendering, and E-Informing.

- **Web-based ERP (Electronic Resource Planning):** The transaction process, from selecting requisitions, purchasing requisitions, placing orders and receiving goods and services, are completed through software systems developed by vendors like SAP and Oracle. These software packages helps to recommend schedules that achieve an ideal production cycle. The software also automatically generates purchase orders of the finished product and forwards supply requests to the suppliers, thus making the final product available more quickly.

- **E-MRO (Maintenance, Repair and Operating):** E-MRO is software that helps to purchase products vital for the repair, maintenance, and operation of machines through the Internet. The software automates important processes, such as selecting requisitions, purchasing requisitions, and the placing and receiving of goods and services. In addition, the software helps to reduce the time taken for repair and maintenance of the products.

- **E-Sourcing:** E-Sourcing, also known as reverse auctioning, involves the use of Internet technology to identify new suppliers for a specific purchasing requirement. A business is able to reach a larger number of suppliers through e-sourcing. With the help of online tools, buyers and suppliers are able to connect quickly and efficiently. E-Sourcing is more effective than the traditional sourcing strategy because it reduces the sourcing cycle time, helps the supplier get rid of labor-intensive processes, and offers more transparency to the process for all involved parties.

- **E-Tendering:** E-Tendering involves the use of Internet technology to send and receive requests for tenders to the suppliers. E-Tendering makes it possible for suppliers located in different geographic locations to bid for a proposal. SmartSuite is an example of e-tendering software, developed by Calsoft. This software allows companies to create online tender and templates, along with publishing tender online.

- **E-Informing:** E-Informing describes the distribution and transfer of information amongst the suppliers that is relevant to Internet purchases and acquisitions. E-Mail is the most common means by which information is exchanged.

E-COLLABORATION

E-Collaboration is defined as the "collaboration, through usage of electronic technologies, among individuals and organizations engaged in a common task"[12]. E-Collaboration facilitates and coordinates decision-making regarding Internet products for both suppliers and customers. E-Collaboration is very important to the e-enabled companies because it helps to maintain real time communication with their supplier(s) about the status and logistics of the product. The most common forms of e-collaboration tools are multimedia and video conferencing, e-mail, and instant messaging.

---

12 www.tamiu.edu/~nedkock/IEEETPC/EcollabSpecIssue.htm

E-Collaboration has become more popular after the emergence of e-collaboration tools offered by companies like Microsoft Corporation and IBM. The collaboration tool by Microsoft, Netmeeting, enables users located in different places to communicate through audio and video conferencing over the Internet. In addition, Netmeeting allows the e-enabled organization to maintain current information about the status of the product with respect to its distribution and logistics.

An example of e-collaboration is the internet-based collaboration of Adaptec[13]. Adaptec uses an e-collaboration tool called "Alliance", which is developed by Extricity. This software enables Adaptec to communicate at any time with its design center, located in California, its foundry in Taiwan, and their numerous assembly plants located in Japan, Singapore, and Hong Kong. Alliance enables the company to exchange details through complex drawings, prototype plans, test results, and production and shipment schedules. The software can help companies reduce the product development cycle and respond quickly to the demand and supply levels.

The placement of the URL of the website and how the product is displayed on the website are both crucial towards attracting more customers. The promotion of a business's products and services through the Internet can be an effective way of attracting attention and creating recognition for their products with new customers. The concept of promotion and how it is accomplished will be the focus of the next chapter.

---

13 www.adaptec.com. It is computer Hardware Company based in Milpitas, California. It produces host adapters for connecting storage devices to computers.

CASE STUDY

Dell was founded by Michael Dell in 1984 in Austin, Texas. Their corporate headquarters is located in Round Rock, Texas. Dell is a global company that has 35,000 employees and operates in 34 countries. Its main geographical divisions are the Americas, Asia –Pacific, Japan, and Europe/Middle East/Africa (EMEA). By 2001, Dell has become one of the largest providers of personal computers. Its business model of direct sales and build-to-order has made it a leader in the domain of personal computers. Through its website, www.dell.com, Dell receives orders online from both individual consumers and businesses all over the world. Dell distributes and delivers their products to many different geographical areas through its efficient supply chain management team and logistics partners.

Dell started selling customizable personal computers over the Internet in 1995. It started with providing customers with technical support and information. Now Dell's website provides real time online order status, an online catalog, technical support, and troubleshooting guides for common problems arising with their products. Dell's service offerings on the website reduce their costs in providing customer care, addressing problems with their products, and managing returns and exchanges. The success of Dell's e-business has allowed Dell to launch PremierDell.com, which gives each customer a website that is a complete record of their relationship with Dell, from order status, management reports and technical support.

To supply their customized products all over the world, Dell has strategically located itself in different parts of the world. These different locations serve to minimize manufacturing and delivery costs, while providing the products to their customers as quickly as possible. Dell also chooses locations that are the most beneficial with respect to labor costs, market access, government incentives, transportation, and information infrastructure. Currently, Dell has manufacturing units in the USA (Texas and Tennessee), Canada, Chile, Mexico, Brazil, Europe (UK and Ireland), New Zealand and Asia Pacific (India, Malaysia, Singapore, Japan, and China).

Dell has many suppliers and partners that are involved in building their customizable products. The various parts of personal computers, like the power adapter, cables, and hard drives, are manufactured by the Dell suppliers who are located in Asia. The finished product is then shipped to the nearest distribution center. The manufacturing unit in the USA has components delivered by suppliers located in Mexico. For example, Flextronics/Solectron and Sanmina-SCI are suppliers who supply motherboard production to the Dell units in USA. Dell has outsourced the production of non-configurable PC, called SmartStep, to Mitac, a Taiwanese company. These suppliers and many other suppliers and partners are linked through Dell's e-procurement system that is subsequently linked to Premier Dell.com.

Customers use the catalog hosted in Dell's website to choose and customize their personal computers. Dell supports supplier's hosted catalog solutions -- like PremierDell.com -- connecting to the e-procurement system of Dell. This is integrated with an ERP application, which supports 20 different industry e-procurement tools. The ERP application of Dell can be integrated with other e-procurement tools like Ariba, SAP, Microsoft, and Oracle. The supplier-hosted solution supports four B2B transactions: Punchout, order requisition, electronic purchase orders and PO acknowledgement. This solution has the advantage of providing real time data updates and data accuracy. It prevents data replication and allows the suppliers of Dell to manage the complexity of different configurations.

Contract manufacturers like Fullertron, a Scottish company, IBM, Lightening Beech (a US company), Trend Tec (a US based company), and APW (an Irish company) manufacture chassis and plastic components based on the specifications provided by Dell. Suppliers like Jabil, SMS, Keytech, located near Dell's manufacturing units, manage the sub-assemblies of products. 65% of the products required by the Ireland manufacturing units are supplied by Dell's suppliers in Asia. Suppliers like Philips, Nokia, Samsung, Sony, and Acer supply specific components and peripherals to European and Asian manufacturing units. Hon-Hao supplies motherboards to manufacturing units in Asia and Europe. The contract manufacturers are directly integrated with the regional head offices of Dell through the e-procurement and e-collaboration softwares.

The supply chain management, especially the e-procurement and e-collaboration of Dell, is managed through the ERP solutions integrated with the suppliers and contract manufacturers. The suppliers, in turn, manage the inventory and complete a particular order based on the specifications and ship it to the distribution hubs. The distribution hubs strategically placed such that the distribution center is located no more than an hour from the supplier facilities. Dell has five distribution hubs to service the European market. These hubs are located in Ireland, UK, Netherlands, Sweden, and South Africa. The information systems in the distribution centers are integrated with the ERP application of the suppliers to maintain inventory control.

CHAPTER SUMMARY

This chapter discussed the place concept and its different features. In addition, this chapter has shown how the development of the Internet has dramatically changed the way products are placed and distributed by the sellers. Companies now have the option of using many different types of technology to support their business, and must decide which technological tool best helps them accomplish their goals. Technologies embedded in e-commerce business models help the customer to buy products no matter where they are. E-Procurement software enables a buyer to procure goods from suppliers all across the world at the best available prices. E-Collaboration software enables the customer, sellers, and suppliers to maintain constant communication for the distribution of products anywhere and anytime.

Place refers to the placement, logistics, and distributions of products through the internet. The distribution of the product is an important part of marketing strategy. This process involves numerous suppliers, manufacturers, exporters, and other distributions channels.

Supply chain management, or SCM, has five components: **Plan** (strategy to execute the SCM program), **Source** (various suppliers), **Make** (the description of the products), **Delivery** (distribution and logistics) and **Return** (customer service).

Place is a part of traditional supply chain management, manifested in the delivery component of SCM. The advancement in Internet technology has given way to the development of a new e-SCM. E-SCM performs the same functions of the traditional SCM, except most are now automated and conducted through e-procurement and e-collaboration software.

There are three main components of place: e-commerce, e-procurement, and e-collaboration. E-Commerce helps to present the products and services of the sellers to the customers through the sellers' websites. Internet transactions, customer service, online advertising and promotion are all conducted through the Internet, electronic data interchange (EDI) and/or value-added networks (VANs). The Internet is the most used and common form through which the business prepares its webpage to lists its products and services.

There are 4 main types of business models: B2B, B2C, C2B and C2C. B2B is the relationship where two businesses can exchange products and services over the Internet. There are 5 types of B2B models: 1) company websites, 2) product supply and procurement exchanges, 3) specialized or vertical business portals, 4) information sites and 5) brokering sites.

B2C is the relationship between a business and consumer. The relationship between consumer and business defines the term C2B. C2C is the transaction between person-to-person. There are many sites which host forums, and auctions, which the consumer uses to buy and sell products.

E-Procurement is the electronic process through which businesses procure components of their products from suppliers to provide the end products and services. There are five types of e-procurement: 1) Web-based ERP, 2) E-Sourcing, 3) E-Tendering, 4) E-MRO, and 5) E-Informing.

E-Collaboration facilitates and coordinates decision making between businesses and consumers. E-Collaboration software has helped businesses shorten their product development cycles while responding quickly to consumer demand and available supply.

REVIEW QUESTIONS

1. Describe the term Place?
2. What are the different components of supply chain management? What part of supply chain management is related to place?
3. How is the traditional supply chain different from E-SCM?
4. What are the different components of Place?
5. What is E-commerce?
6. Explain, using examples, the different business models of e-commerce?
7. What is the B2B business model? Describe the various types of business models with examples?
8. What is e-procurement and what is its importance in placing the products?
9. What are the different types of e-procurement?
10. Explain the term e-collaboration?

REFERENCES

1. Dewan, R, M. Freimer, A. Seidmann(2000), *"Organizing Distribution Channels for Information Goods on the Internet"*, Management Science, 46, 4, 483-494.
2. C2B business model (2005); accessed on 14-4-2008. http:// c2b.typepad.com/c2b/2005/08/the_c2b_revolut.html
3. E-procurement solutions (200http://www.bestpricecomputers. co.uk/glossary/e-procurement.htm
4. SiliconFeast (2005); *Supply Chain Management*; accessed on 17-4-2008; http://www.siliconfareast.com/supply-chain.htm
5. http://www.verticalportals.com/

6. http://www.webmd.com/

7. http://www.esa-thevoice.org/ecoll.html

8. A.T. Kearny (2008); E-sourcing http://www.atkearneyprocurementsolutions.com/solutions/faq.html

9. http://projects.bus.lsu.edu/independent_study/vdhing1/b2c/

10. E.COM by Ravi Kalakota and Andrew Winsten

11. http://www.calsoftes.com/smartsuite/e-tendering-software.html0

12. http://www.srmarketing.com/Tutorial-ImpactofInformationrevolution.html

13. http://www.rowan.edu/business/FACULTY/dosoglu/ch01/index.htm

14. Business Models for Electronic Markets by Paul Timmers, Electronic Markets, Vol. 8, No. 2, 1998.

15. Johnson, E and Whang S (2002); *E-business and Supply chain Management; an Overview and Framework; Production and operation management;* Vol 11 No.4.

16. Auctions on the Internet: What's Being Auctioned, and How? by David Lucking -Reiley, Journal of Industrial Economics, forthcoming, September 2000, Source: http://www.vanderbilt.edu/econ/reiley/papers/InternetAuctions.pdf

17. Kraemer, Kenneth and Dedrick, J; Dell Computer: Organization of a global Production Network. Accessed on 18-4-2008; www.crito.uci.edu/git/publications/pdf/**dell**.pdf

18. http://www.indiainfoline.com/bisc/ieec.html

19. www.makethemove.com

20. http://www.computinginsights.com/Topic1.html

21. http://www.apqc.org/PresFiles/smith/tsld052.htm

22. http://www.ketera.com/newsletter/bp_031307_story1.html

CHAPTER 8

PROMOTION

Chapter Contents

- Objectives
- Introduction
- Advantages and Disadvantages of Internet Promotion
- Types of Internet Promotion
- Technology for Online Ads
    1. Methods of Targeting Online Ads
    2. Methods of Delivery
    3. Rich Media
- Criticism Against Online Promotion
- Future of Online Promotions
- Case Study
    Success through Viral Marketing – A Case Study on Unilever's AXE
- Chapter Summary
- Review Questions
- References

"Welcome to the performance economy where marketers who know their daily conversion rate, conversion per campaign, online revenue per campaign and online revenue per conversion will thrive, while those who don't get it will die on the vine."[42]

- Larry Cleary, President & Chief Operating Officer, Inceptor(TM), Inc.

OBJECTIVES

This chapter gives a basic introduction to promotion, its meaning, history, definitions, and its importance to a successful marketing strategy. The multitude of styles and the growth of advertising on the Internet will be covered, including the use of Internet advertising for non-intent related products. The chapter illustrates the successful promotion Unilever used to position its product, AXE, in today's market.

INTRODUCTION

The previous chapter explained some of the dynamics involved in the placement of products online and the different tools available to companies to accomplish product placement effectively. The Internet has created new opportunities for companies to market and promote their products. Besides being a powerful communication and promotional tool, the Internet has also ensured effective measurement of the promotional methods. The Internet also offers the convenience of customizing the promotion for the customers. This gives companies a better understanding of the preferences of their consumers and allows them to communicate more effectively with them. These new methods of marketing in many ways have been more effective than the

42 Hollis Thomases, "The Future of Online Marketing", E-marketing – The Emerging Trends, Icfai University Press, 2002

traditional methods. Interestingly, several businesses known for their traditional practices considered marketing their products and services on the Internet.

The first ads on the Internet appeared during the mid-1990s. Thereafter, the Internet was looked at as an effective and novel medium to promote products and services. Advertisers operating either in global or niche markets have benefited from advertising on the Internet. Certain websites thrive only by selling their advertising space.

ADVANTAGES AND DISADVANTAGES OF INTERNET PROMOTION

There are several advantages to product promotion on the Internet. For instance, ads can be customized and targeted to the right audience at a lower cost. However, advertising on the Internet also has its share of disadvantages. For instance, privacy issues and data theft problems are prevalent on the Internet, and can be very damaging to businesses. In addition, the advertiser must maintain the interest of the consumer completely through Internet advertising, which is a very difficult task. Despite the disadvantages, the advantages of Internet promotion cannot be ignored and Internet promotion is becoming increasingly popular.

Advantages

1. **Cost Effectiveness**: Product promotion on the Internet is cost effective. Compared to other forms of promotion, companies will spend much less on Internet promotion. Companies no longer have to spend money on producing and distributing physical advertisements, and can reduce their expenditures for TV or radio advertisements. Promotional costs on the

Internet are just a small fraction of what it would cost using traditional method of advertising.

2. **Market Expansion:** Promotional activities through the Internet can create and open up access to new markets that businesses would not have previously thought of. This leads to more companies expanding and strengthening their distribution facilities to cater to customers from different geographical markets. This results in companies having a greater global presence and consumers having more purchase options.

3. **Market Penetration:** Websites allow companies to remain open during all hours and provide greater visibility to the business and its products/services at a relatively low cost. This opens up more opportunities for the customers to gather information about the products and make their product decision. Therefore, companies can easily penetrate into several demographic and geographic markets more effectively and more efficiently.

4. **Faster Access:** Promotion on the Internet means instant communication with the intended audience. Customers can easily establish a contact with the company, which can be further used for facilitating purchase and feedback. Therefore, companies can gain a significant competitive advantage by using blogs, pop-up ads and other online promotional tools. This ensures greater awareness of products/services and

brands for consumers. In addition, faster access can contribute to stronger long-term relationships between the business and its customers.

5. **Saves Time**: A website that is creatively designed not only helps in directing consumers to its website, but also effectively provides all important product information. The website generally includes basic information about the products, in-depth descriptions, pictures, common uses, purchase options and where it can be serviced. The company can also include a section on Frequently Asked Questions (FAQs). FAQs are a good, low-cost way for companies to provide additional information about common problems consumers may have with specific products. FAQs save time for both the sellers and the customers.

6. **Enduring Content:** Internet advertising endures for a greater duration of time than traditional advertising methods. For example, advertising in a newspaper or magazine is only effective for the short period of time before the next issues come out. Internet promotions can generate sales for much longer periods of time. In addition, promotions can be constantly altered or changed on the Internet for significantly lower costs than traditional advertising methods.

7. **Measurement of Promotional Activities:** One of the biggest advantages of Internet promotions is the ability to measure the effectiveness of the promotional

tools. For example, there are tracking devices that allow businesses to monitor how many first-time visitors and repeat visitors are accessing their promotions on the website. This provides marketers with more information about what the best promotional strategies are to attract more customers.

Disadvantages

1. **Lack of 'Touch and Feel'**: Despite having attractive, customer-friendly websites, companies cannot be guaranteed sales because the physical feel of the product is absent. For some customers, this absence of the ability to physically test or examine a product will prevent them from ultimately purchasing the product. For this reason, companies cannot rely solely on Internet promotion. This is also true in developed markets, where several companies are selling similar products and services. The lack of product differentiation, coupled with customer inability to physically examine the product, makes Internet sales more difficult and Internet promotions less effective.

2. **Lack of Personal Touch:** Throughout the Internet sales process, the customers and the salespersons are isolated. This may reduce the possibility of developing a relationship between the customer and the business. Hence marketers have to devise programs to keep the customers engaged even after the sale.

3. Threat of Internet Crime: With theft becoming more prevalent on the Internet, companies must adopt methods to protect their customers' credit card information from being stolen. Another disadvantage of Internet promotion is the possibility of important personal information of customers being stolen. This might discourage some customers from customers purchasing online.

TYPES OF INTERNET PROMOTION

There are several methods of promoting on the Internet. They come in various shapes, sizes and technologies.

1) **Search Engines:** The most common method of searching for information on the Internet is through search engines. Therefore, the first place for businesses to promote their products and services on the Internet is to use search engines. With the availability and popularity of search engines like Google and Yahoo!, Internet users use them to locate their destination websites. Based on the search terms they input, the search engine displays a list that not only contains the address of the website but also other related sites. Search engines also provide sponsored links along with the list. These sponsored links are paid for by the advertisers.

2) **E-Mail Publishing:** E-mail publishing is a way to engage prospective customers who have shown interest by visiting a company's website. The best way to establish the relationship is to offer information by

asking to send an email or request that the visitor to sign up for a free newsletter. Once the trust is built, and the potential customer knows that the newsletter or any other information is not necessarily an inducement to make a purchase, customers will now have gained the name and brand recognition for the company. Over time, the company can target these potential customers with direct offers and other promotions to generate sales.

3) **Viral Strategies:** In traditional marketing circles, word-of mouth is considered to be the most effective form of promotion. This involves customers spreading information about products and services to other people, creating interest in the product. The Internet has brought about 'word-of-mouse', or viral marketing, as a strategy that encourages others to spread the marketing message through e-mail. The most widely quoted example is that of Hotmail.com. Each e-mail carries a message to the recipient to sign up for a hotmail account. Similarly, several online greeting card businesses have their marketing messages displayed when a sender sends a card from the site. The recipient is also encouraged to reciprocate by sending a 'thank you' card to the sender (Exhibit I).

Principles of Viral Marketing

It is believed that viral marketers practice delayed gratification. They can generate a substantial amount of interest and accrue profits in the future. Following are some of the basic principles of viral marketing.

- Gives away valuable prodcucts or services – Most of the viral marketing strategies offer products for free. This helps in attracting the attention. It is observed that anything that is offered for free attracts people. Over a period of time it also helps to sell the product. Apart from sales in the future, companies can receive e-mail addresses from potential customers, create a database of customers, target ads and products and generate several other opportunities for sale.

- Provides for effortless transfer to others – Viral marketing strategies work better when they are transferred effortlessly and at lower cost. Internet offers itself as the most suitable medium. It also helps in transmitting the marketing message instantaneously. Further, it can be downloaded and copied. Thus viral marketing aids easy transfer of messages.

- Scales easily from small to very large – Scalability has to be built in the viral strategy. The number has to grow rapidly from small to big and it needs to be supported by other plans and strategies.

- Exploits common motivation and behaviors – Viral marketing, to be successful, needs to identify the common factors of motivation. Like for instance, greed, the urge to be different are some reasons that drive people to react in a particular manner.

- Utilizes existing communication networks – It is important that viral messages are transmitted within the existing networks. With each person having 8-12 people in their network of friends and family, the message would further be transferred.

- Takes advantage of others' resources – It is not necessary that the marketer needs to have his own website to spread his message. Affiliate programs help in placing the viral message on other websites. It helps in two ways. One, another website relaying the message and not the advertiser himself. Two, resources of the other website are depleted and not that of the advertiser.

Exhibit I: Principles of Viral Marketing

Source: Dr. Ralph F Wilson, "The Six Principles of Viral Marketing", E-marketing The Emerging Trends, Icfai University Press, 2002

There are several methods through which a company can spread information about its products online. For example, the company can sponsor online discussion groups, blogs, or promote the product in chat rooms. Small businesses can publish articles that talk about their businesses or any other trends in the market and publish them on another website. This provides a larger forum for readers to learn more about their company.

4) **Promotion by Placing Links:** If a website has more links directing web users towards it, this will result in increased viewing of the website. Usually links can be placed in complementary sites. At the same time, the marketer has to create content good enough that will

maintain the customer's attention after being linked to it.

Typically, links can be placed on websites that cover industry information or on the sites of associations that the company belongs to. It is also quite common to create links through banner exchanges. Company A can agree to place Company B's banner on their website in exchange for placing their banner on Company B's website.

Promotion on the Internet using links is also possible by paying affiliates for the sales generated through the links placed on their sites. This will be covered more extensively under paid advertising.

5) **Traditional Media**: Similar to the role that PR plays in Internet promotion, it is also crucial to use traditional media to augment all website promotions. Paid advertising, in the form of a small display ad in a newspaper or magazine, directing readers to visit the company's website, can also help generate additional sales.

6) **Public Relations**: Although companies may have a presence on the Internet, it is also important to get enough press coverage for the website. A news release, when published on the Internet or through print media, can direct Internet users to the website. Since PR is not paid for, it acts as free promotion for the website.

However, marketers need to use PR tools effectively by promoting the most attractive features and events the company has to offer. Marketers need to be prepared for unbiased editorial comments about the company as well as event promotion.

7) **Networking:** Networking is another important tool that can help gain more product recognition for the company and attract more customers. Networking is generally accomplished through news groups or discussion lists. In a discussion list, people use the Internet to discuss specific topics. Regular interactions between the company and customers build trust and also foster long-term relationships. These forums are the best platforms for viral marketing, because it allows companies to distribute information about their products and services in an efficient and effective manner.

8) **Paid Advertising:** The above discussed promotional tools are generally developed in-house at a lesser cost. However, businesses can also seek the help of professional agencies that have the expertise to promote on the Internet. These agencies specialize in Internet advertising and are better served to determine the best advertising methods for specific companies. Some paid advertising methods include:

A. **Banner Advertising** – Banner ads were the first method of Internet product promotion. Banner ads are usually animated and are linked to some other website. They could either appear at the top of the website, or pop-up on certain pages when a specific word is keyed in or a certain page is accessed.

B. **Skyscrapers** – Skyscrapers are banner ads but they occupy a greater amount of space on the website. Skyscrapers became popular when banner ads started to become monotonous and lost effectiveness with the average customer. Ad designers on the Internet began to experiment by placing vertical strips of text and images on the sides of webpages, and this differentiated form of skyscraper advertising has experienced some success.

C. **Interstitial** – These are full-page ads that appear when the user enters or exits a website. They appear when the page is loading or closing and last from 5 to 15 seconds. The time lag between the closing of one webpage and the loading of another page is used to display the ad message. These ads close on their own after the new page is loaded . Sometimes the web user is given the option to skip these ads or go to the intended webpage by clicking on the provided hyperlink.

D. **Pop-Up Windows** – Pop-up ads can appear whenever a webpage is loaded, displaying the advertisement. Clicking on the window takes the user to the advertiser's website. These windows can also be closed if the user is not interested in the ad. Advertisers began to use pop-ups when they realized that web users rarely clicked on banner ads or even looked at them. The presentation of pop-ups forces web users to scroll or read through the advertisement prior to closing the ad.

E. **Pop-Under Ads:** Another variation of pop-ups is the pop-under ads. These ads do not interrupt the browsing activity of the surfer. Pop-under ads are visible as a separate window only when the web user closes the window of the website that has triggered the ad.

F. **Pay-Per-Sale Advertising** – This is also known as the Affiliate or Associate program. The company can enter into agreements to place links to their website on the websites of several affiliates. For every sale through the link, the affiliate site/company earns a commission, which is usually 5 to 15% of the sale.

G. **Opt-in-E-Mail Advertising** – This is also known as permission marketing, which states that there is better customer response if a marketing message is sent to a willing potential customer. Therefore, companies will send e-mail marketing messages to individuals who have opted in to receive them. These opt-in-e-mail advertising arrangements are more successful because e-mails to unwilling or unknown customers may end up being viewed unfavorably and will thwart all measures to build trust with potential customers (Exhibit II).

The Three Pillars of Permission Marketing

- Anticipated for acceptance (Cut through the clutter)
- Personalized for relevance (Empower customers with choice)
- Trusted for dependence (Shift decision-making power to marketers)

Exhibit II: The Three Pillars of Permission Marketing

Source: Allen S.F.; 'Don't Call Yourself a Permission Marketer When You are a Direct Marketer'; http://www.dancingflower.com/pm/pm.html

H. Online Advergaming: Teenagers and young adults are the most frequent users of online games. Businesses try to appeal to teenagers and young adults by advertising through video, audio, and animated characters. This market has further captivated the imagination of marketers, who have used online games to embed their marketing messages.

I. Paid Listings in Portal Sites – On a portal site of an educational institution, an ad for a website selling educational materials can be listed. For every sale through this type of website, a proceed of the sale is given to the educational institution. This form of promotion is termed as paid listings in portal sites.

J. Paid Ads in Targeted E-Mail Newsletters – Newsletters can also carry advertising messages for a fee. It is estimated that the click through rates are in the range of 1 to 3%.

K. Leaderboard Ads - Leaderboard ads are text ads placed on the webpage. They resemble rectangular box items with links to a destination site.

L. Pay-per-click Links – Pay-per-click links are usually placed on search engines. The price per click for the link depends upon competitive pricing (Exhibit III).

M. Sponsorships – Sponsorships are paid ads on websites or e-mail newsletters. They are usually on a long-term basis.

Metrics in Internet Advertising

Irrespective of how a company wants to promote, either through tradition methods or on the Internet, the promotional strategy needs to be monitored and measured for effectiveness. Following are some of the metrics used in Internet advertising.

Click-Through Rate (CTR): When banners are placed on other websites, the visitors of the website may click on the banner to reach the advertiser's destination website. This process of clicking through an online advertisement is known as CTR. The CTR measures the percentage of visitors who have clicked against the total number who have visited the webpage.

It is possible that a visitor to the webpage might not click on the banner but reach the URL of the advertiser directly. Therefore, CTR cannot measure the overall response to the ad, but only the immediate response.

Cost-per-click (CPC): CPC measures the user's interaction with the ad. The interaction can occur in the form of click-through, in-click or mouse-over. When the interaction is through in-click and mouse-over, the user remains within the ad and not reaches the destination website.

Cost-per-action (CPA): This forms the basis of payment for the visitor's reaction. Hence it becomes important that there is some conversion.

Cost-per-thousand-impression (CPM): A single instance of an online ad on a webpage is known as an impression. This forms the basis of payment for online ads.

Pay-per-click (PPC): This is another payment model which is based on click-through for an online ad on a webpage. For every click, the payment is made and not necessarily for conversion.

Pay-per-sale (PPS): In this method, payment is based on sale through user interaction of the online ad. This seems to be an effective method. However, if the user does not make the sale, it neither benefits the publisher of the online ad not the advertiser.

Conversion rate: Typically any promotional strategy begins with a certain set of objectives. All the objectives are desired actions like sale of the product, downloading software, subscribing for the newsletter, membership registration, asking for more information, etc. Conversion arête depends upon the attitude of the customer, the level of interest shown, the offer, and the convenience with which the purchase can be made.

Cost-per-lead (CPL): The advertiser pays based on the leads generated at the destination site. A lead involves some contact information provided by the user, like signing up for newsletters or registration. It could also be demographic information provided by the user.

Cost-per-download (CPD): The payment is made to the publisher of the online ad when the user downloads software or documents. This download action is possible only after the user interacts with the ad.

Exhibit III: Metrics in Internet Advertising

Source: Ojha A C, "Online AD Technologies", Internet Advertising – An Introduction, Icfai University Press, 2006

TECHNOLOGY FOR ONLINE ADS

The Internet is becoming a more viable medium to promote products and services because of the increasing availability of advertising technologies. Furthermore, the constant improvement of technology has led marketers to be able to improve the quality of their online ads. Some of these sophisticated technologies include DHTML, animated GIF images, and rich media. In addition, technologies that track the online user's behavior have further increased the effectiveness of online advertisements.

1. Methods of Targeting Online Advertising

The Internet provides ample opportunity for advertisers to target their ads to the right audience. An online ad that is targeted to the desired group of customers significantly increases its effectiveness. Businesses must select the appropriate targeting method to find the right group of customers to address their advertising to. The following methods are some of the major approaches to targeting:

Demographic Targeting: Demographic targeting is similar to the demographic grouping method used in traditional promotion. Under this method, consumers are classified based on gender, income, age, location, and other demographic variables. Technology is now available which lets the ad server to read the Internet Protocol (IP) address of the user's computer and record the location information. The ad server can also use a cookie, which is a piece of information sent from an ad server to the user's desktop which is read back by the ad server. The cookie identifies the user when he visits the website again. This can assist the ad server in placing the right advertisements to target this user.

Behavioral Targeting: Ad strategies can be implemented based on the observed behavior of the web user. The types of behavioral information that can be deduced based on the habits of the web user are the type of pages browsed, time spent on each webpage and items clicked on each page. Usually, cookies are used to keep track of the browsing habits of the web user.

Contextual Targeting: It is very important that the right ad is delivered to the user. To ensure that the ads used have a better chance of being appealing to the web user, the context of where the ad is placed needs to be determined. For instance, an ad promoting greeting cards is not likely to be effective on a webpage that details the textile industry. Such irrelevant placing of ads is not only ineffective, but also can be considered a nuisance by the user. Ad technologies use their tracking information to find and deliver contextually relevant ads.

Keyword Targeting: Whenever the user keys in certain words in the Search box of the website, the server looks for matching documents that contain one or more words specified by the user. It is observed that when users search for products or services, they enter the required name of the product and/or service or the brand name as the keyword in to the Search box. Based on this observation, online ad technologies track the keywords used and deliver the appropriate ad to the user.

2. Methods of Delivery

Depending on the method of delivery, online ads can be classified as server-side ad technology or Client-side Ad Technology. Server-side ad technology relies on ad servers to deliver the ad through the web browser. The ad server also rotates the ads from the ad inventory. The rotation of ads may be random or based on certain criteria. In addition, the ad server tracks the performance of the ad and provides the performance information to the advertiser. The ad server is either maintained by the website or a third party provider. There are several products that provide server-side ad technology, such as Banner Fusion, Unicast, Open AdStream, Juggler, and AdRotator.

Client-side Ad Technology uses software called Adware. Whenever a user downloads free software from the Internet, the adware is also downloaded onto the user's computer. The adware consists of ads that are displayed on the user's desktop.

3. Rich Media

Internet technology has developed drastically, enabling the improvement of bandwidth. Improvements in bandwidth allow online advertisers to make ads using available rich media, which makes the advertisements more interactive and effective. Rich media combines animation, video and sound to deliver the ad message in an interactive fashion. Ads that use rich media are dynamic in nature or respond through action when the user clicks on the ad. The most popular type of rich media is the Macromedia Flash. The rich media ads can be embedded in a page or downloaded. Rich media ads are available as floating ads, rollovers, expandable ads and Flash Ads. Research has also revealed that rich media ads result in increased brand awareness from users and greater sales.

CRITICISMS AGAINST ONLINE PROMOTION

Online promotions have become popular since the mid-1990s. Several websites came onto the scene and used artificial means to influence the number of visits to their websites. During this initial period of online promotions, there were no suitable mechanisms to verify the effectiveness of the ads. Several websites manipulated figures about the visitor numbers through software programs. Finally, when the dot-com bubble burst, several websites that used these methods to lure advertisers collapsed. This, however, cautioned advertisers to look at realistic figures about online promotion (Exhibit IV).

Virtual Shoplifting

Though pay-per-click online promotions are considered to be effective, click thieves from within their homes and offices can indulge in shoplifting on the Internet. They click on the pay per click ads without showing any intention to buy the products or services.

Sometimes the click thieves are hired by ad publishers or affiliate partners of PPC search engines. It helps them to inflate the click figures to charge more from the advertiser. Further, these figures are used to claim high traffic to their sites and also to justify the high prices charged.

Ad publishers or affiliates could also create an automated program, like Google Clique which automatically clicked on paid ads while remaining undetected by search engines.

Exhibit IV: Virtual Shoplifting

Source: Dmitri Eroshenko, "Click Fraud", Internet Advertising – An Introduction, Icfai University Press, 2006

Another criticism of online promotions is that the confidential information of users can be compromised, leading to unsolicited promotional material that is a nuisance to web users. Companies purchase e-mail addresses of web users from service providers. These companies, in turn, send unsolicited promotional mail, known as spam. Spam mail is very difficult to prevent.

Furthermore, promotion on the Internet might not be ideal for all types of products. Although promotion on the Internet is considered to be effective for high-involvement products that require detailed descriptions, it is difficult to market low-involvement products for which consumers do not require a great deal of information.

FUTURE OF ONLINE PROMOTIONS

Internet promotions can end up being very successful. However, businesses must approach online advertising pragmatically. For instance, banner ads are no longer effective and businesses should look to go in a different direction. In addition, there will be increased demand from advertisers for ads on the pay-per-performance model. Similarly, there will likely be more of an emphasis on geo-targeted advertising and contextual advertising. E-mail marketers must adhere to legislation and limit the amount of spam mail they send to prospective customers.

Over time, online businesses have begun to share the lists of their registered members with each other in a cross-promotional effort. This serves to reduce costs in finding prospective customers for each business. In addition, there has been significant activity towards the co-branding of online companies. The next level for marketers is likely to sustain the relationships built with their customers through effective utilization of Electronic Customer Relationship Management (E-CRM).

Despite the concerns raised against online promotion, it has expanded the markets for advertisers. This chapter has shown the efforts of online ad agencies in innovating new forms of online ads and increasing the effectiveness of the ads. In addition, this chapter has discussed the tools available for promoting a product and the importance of promotion in marketing strategy. In the current Internet marketplace, the most effective form of promotion is personalization of advertisement. Creating a personal connection between the business and the customer is the most direct and effective way for firms to attract and retain customers. Personalization is the focus of the next chapter. Based on recent market trends, online ads are becoming more and more necessary for companies looking to attract new customers and expand their business.

CASE STUDY

Success through Viral Marketing – A Case Study on Unilever's
AXE

The US deodorant market in 2003 was led by four companies – P&G, Gillette (later taken over by P&G), Unilever and Colgate Palmolive. Each company held a market share slightly above 10%. P&G led the market with approximately 25% market share. There were several private brands that dotted the landscape of the market.

The male deodorant market has also witnessed a change over the years. Men in the US have shown an increasing interest in male grooming products. During this period, Unilever, whose market share had dropped to 5.4% in 2001, launched AXE (in 2002). AXE was already a successful brand in other markets. It was also the second largest global deodorant brand. Unilever intended to take some of the market share away from P&G by recreating the success of AXE in US. Within two years of its launch, in 2004, AXE was the leading brand in the $1.3 billion US deodorant market. It had a market share of 80%. By 2005, it was the fastest growing brand in the deodorant category with over $100 million in sales.

Industry observers believed that AXE's success was due to its clever and unconventional Internet marketing. Following the success of AXE, P&G launched Red Zone through its brand Old Spice in 2004, while Gillette launched TAG in 2005. The competition intensified when P&G, to reinvigorate Old Spice, launched an online initiative, Voice of Experience through www.oldspice.com. This was closely on the heels of the success of AXE's viral marketing strategy.

AXE's Launch in the U.S. Market

Unilever first launched AXE in France in 1983. It went on to become a success. Two years later, it was launched in UK. Within the next seven years, it attained a market share of 17%. It was also launched in other European and Latin American markets. It continued to succeed and achieve market shares over 10%. In 1999, AXE made a foray into the Mexican market. In a span of three years, it captured 10% of the market.

Unilever affirmed that AXE was not an ordinary deodorant. It gave the benefit of 24 hours odor control for an affordable price between $4-5 for a 4 oz spray canister. The product had an attractive packaging in black. It was offered in eight different fragrances: Phoenix, Voodoo,

Kilo, Apollo, Essence, Orion, Touch and Tsunami. It was targeted at 18 to 34 year old men. However, Unilever realized very soon that AXE was also popular with 11 to 13 year old boys. AXE was distributed through drug stores and mass outlets. Unilever used specially created in-store merchandising and placed the product in highly visible parts of the stores.

During its product launch, Unilever focused on advertising AXE through television. The ads contained a common theme: using AXE makes men irresistible to women. The company also attracted attention by promoting AXE in malls. They used female models dressed as 'AXE Angels', who sprayed young male visitors with AXE.

However, Unilever quickly realized that traditional TV advertising was not achieving the results they wanted. Research also showed that 95% of the target market was spending more time online. This led to the company launching promotional initiatives on the Internet.

Early Promotional Initiatives on the Internet

Initially, Unilever placed banner ads on the websites of magazines primarily catering to male audiences, such as Maxim, FHM and AtomFilms. The banners directed the traffic to the AXE website (launched in 2002). The website showcased commercials which were considered inappropriate for the television audience. It was expected that the website would have 100,000 visits during the first month, but it drew seven times the expected figure. Within four months, the website registered 1.7 million visits.

When Unilever launched its web-based promotional activities, it expected the target audience to discover the brand themselves and spread positive feedback about the AXE brand amongst their peers. Finally, when the website had experienced more web visitors than was initially expected, it turned out that nearly one-third of the 1.7 million visits were from those who were referred to the site by friends.

The launch campaign of AXE went on to gain a great deal of praise, the foremost being the Business 2.0 Sweet Spot Award for being the most innovative and successful marketing campaign in 2003.

AXE House Party

During December 2002, Unilever announced an extravagant house party through a radio campaign. The radio ad pushed young men to register at www.axehouseparty.com (launched in 2003). The visitors had to participate in an online video game and win invitations to the party (Exhibit A). To support the campaign further, fliers were posted in night clubs and print ads were carried in magazines like Spin and Rolling Stones. The selected winners were flown in, along with young girls, to attend the party at a mansion in the suburbs of Miami. The party featured the latest music, TV and celebrities.

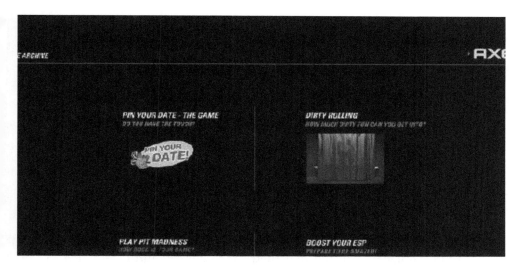

Exhibit A: Online Games on AXE Website

Source: www.axehouseparty.com/axearchive.html

The party received special promotion on television. It was aired for an hour on 'The New TNN' channel. It was also talked about on popular TV shows, magazines, and websites. The promotional event, which was a mix of traditional advertising, web-based promotion and an unconventional event, resulted in an increase of brand awareness by 22%. The brand also reported an increase of 3-3.7% in market share in the 11-24 year age category. Unilever further took advantage of the popularity of the event by offering a complimentary CD that contained the music featured in the party, along with two free bottles of AXE.

Promotional Initiatives in 2005

During 2005, AXE faced a slight slump in its sales. This resulted in the brand moving to the second position in the US deodorant market. This led Unilever to launch a new product in 2005, AXE Unlimited. Unilever's launch of this new fragrance variant coincided with the launch of an online game, Mojo Master. The company intended to combine the two product launches and promote Axe Unlimited through viral marketing.

Mojo Master was a fantasy game targeted at young men. The players had to visit the website, MojoMastergame.com and display their playboy skills when encountered with women at various locations in New York and Los Angeles. In the following months, the game was to be upgraded with more women and locations. The Mojo Master website also carried a blog titled EvanandGareth.com, which detailed the experiences of two men, Evan and Gareth. The blog featured video clips of these two men's encounters with women during their trek across the US. Unilever expected that these video clips would be emailed to young men, creating a ripple effect in favor of the AXE brand.

Way Ahead

It was estimated that the male grooming market in the US would grow to $1.64 billion in 2008 (from $1.3 billion in 2004). Within a short period, 2000 to 2004, the market had grown by 258%. At the same time, the marketplace was becoming competitive with several brands and similar Internet promotional strategies being launched by rival P&G. Can AXE sustain its position in the US market? Should it continue to focus on viral marketing?

CHAPTER SUMMARY

Promotion on the Internet is not just another option for advertisers any more. Initially, the Internet promotions came only from online businesses. Over time, several traditional players have realized that Internet promotions are becoming more and more necessary. Currently, Internet promotions have gained enough prominence to be part of the overall media mix for business advertisers.

Promotion on the Internet began in the 1990s with banner ads. This was soon followed by changes in the way ads appeared and were placed on websites. Banner ads were replaced in popularity by pop-up ads and interstitials. Another significant factor that has fueled the popularity of Internet promotion is the development of superior Internet technology. Better technology has not only made ads more effective, but also has helped companies to better measure the effectiveness of their advertising. Businesses can now track the number of visits to their website and target specific individuals who are repeat visitors to their website.

The greatest innovation in Internet promotion has been the use of Rich Media in advertising. Rich Media offers users an opportunity to interact with the ad message. This has further led to the development of new ad forms such as Advergaming. On the other hand, marketers have gone so far as to create games on their websites allowing customers to explore the game and receive the brand message. Another online ad that has caught the attention of the marketers is the use of viral marketing strategies. Viral strategy is the replica of word-of-mouth, but here the difference lies in the spreading of the message through the Internet. Viral strategy could be as simple as forwarding an e-mail containing the message.

The use of technology in online promotion has also resulted in effective segmentation of the online customers. Customers on the Internet can be targeted based on geographic variables, demographic factors, behavior on the Internet, context, and keywords used in a search engine. Therefore, technology has enabled effective segmentation of web users, which leads to more effective targeting of consumers with specific advertising.

However, Internet promotion is not free from issues relating to privacy and ethics. Several publishers use unfair means to demonstrate that their websites are more popular than they actually are, in efforts to solicit payment from advertisers. In addition, marketers have also shared list of subscribers, resulting in the spread of private information about consumers. Despite these issues, Internet promotions are becoming more popular in the marketplace and viewed as necessary to overall business success.

REVIEW QUESTIONS

1. Discuss the relative advantages/disadvantages of promotion on the Internet?

2. Can a company use traditional forms of advertising to direct traffic to its website?
   Explain.

3. Explain online Advergaming. Illustrate how companies have used online games to promote their products*/* and/or services?

4. Referring to the AXE case study, explain how some of the principles of viral marketing apply to AXE's viral marketing strategy?

5. How is technology shaping the future of promotions on the Internet? Explain.

REFERENCES

1. Aich Vasudha, *"Unilever's Viral Marketing for AXE"*, *Internet Advertising – An Introduction*, Icfai University Press, 2006

2. Antionette Alexander, *"Media, Euro Influence Drive Growth. Helps Men's Grooming Carve Solid Niche"*, www.findarticles.com, September 2004

3. Vavra Bob, *"An Axe to Grind"*, www.ebsco.com, January 2002

4. Thomas Mucha, *"Spray Here, Get Girl"*, www.Business2.com, June 2003

5. Jack Neff, *"Axe Board Helps Find 'Whack Jack'"*, www.ebsco.com, October 2004

6. Theresa Howard, *"A Nice Smelling Man is Hard to Find"*, www.usatoday.com, July 2005

7. Wilson F. Dr. Ralph, *"The Eight Essential Types of Internet Promotion"*, www.wilsonweb.com, June 2000

8. Lendor Carla, *"Internet Promotion – Advantages and*

Disadvantages", www.ezinearticles.com

9. Hollis Thomases, "*The Future of Online Marketing*", *E-marketing – The Emerging Trends*", Icfai University Press, 2002

10. K Suresh, "Online *Advertising – A Critical Look*", *Internet Advertising – An Introduction*", Icfai University Press, 2006

11. Dmitri Eroshenko, "*Click Fraud*", *Internet Advertising – An Introduction*, Icfai University Press, 2006

12. Dr. Ralph F Wilson, "*The Six Principles of Viral Marketing*", *E-marketing – The Emerging Trends*, Icfai University Press, 2006

PERSONALIZATION

Chapter Contents

- Objectives
- Introduction
- Personalization vs. Customization
- Personalization vs. Customer Relationship Marketing
- Importance of Personalization
- Personalized Services
  1. Personalization in Entertainment Industry
  2. Personalization in Publication Industry
- Technologies
  1. Neural Networks
  2. Collaborative Filtering
  3. Forms
  4. Click-stream Analysis
  5. Expert Systems and Rule-based Engine
- Consumer
- Privacy
- Case Study
- Chapter Summary
- Review Questions
- References

CHAPTER 9

OBJECTIVES

The objective of this chapter is to give a basic introduction to personalization, its meaning and definitions. The difference between customer relationship building in the brick and mortar context and online customer relationship building will be covered in this chapter. This chapter also covers the different phases of personalization, including customer interactions, customer profiles, analysis of these profiles and other customer data, and targeting of marketing activities to suit the customer profile. The chapter ends with a case study of Amazon.com.

INTRODUCTION

Personalization refers to the practice of individualizing the marketing content and programs for one customer based on a customer's unique profile. Personalization can also be characterized as "building customer loyalty by building a meaningful one-to-one relationship"[43]. It is often compared to "a delightful experience….like walking into a restaurant and being greeted by name or having your favorite book given to you by your bookseller"[44]. Remembering customer names, needs, and preferences helps sellers retain customers and maintain a competitive edge with respect to their customers. Personalization is an advanced form of promotion, where the products and services are customized to fit the individual customer. The last chapter discussed the importance of promoting a product based on the market segment. This chapter addresses personalization and the way it is accomplished in e-commerce.

In the traditional retail market, shopkeepers call their regular customers by name and recommend items to them based on their

---

43 Riecken, D. (ed.) Personalized Views of Personalization, Communications of the ACM, 43 (8), August 2000, 27-28
44 SIGIA-L mailing list archive http://www.listquest.com/lq/search.html?ln=sigia

past shopping history. In the same way, personalization in the online world addresses customers individually and attempts to relate to them personally. Web users register on a website and create a profile that gives a detailed account of their interests, hobbies, and preferences. The website also records information like visit history, webpages viewed, and duration of these viewings. Based on this information, the site administrator sends emails to customers, notifying them of special promotions, deals and vouchers.

The aim of personalization is to improve the experience of the consumer and create higher customer satisfaction during their website visit. Personalization is basically a one-to-one relationship between a seller and visitor. The seller creates a visitor profile, which is a collection of attributes derived from the web user's web activity. Based on the visitor profile, the sellers target their promotional product in a way that creates the feeling of personalized service to the customer. The seller compiles matching visitor profiles to make a visitor segment, similar to the concept of market segmentation in traditional marketing. The visitor segment consists of all the registered users of the website of the vendors, and the information that is gathered during the interactions of these users.

Segmentation of visitor profiles helps the sellers to identify the type of customers that are generally using the website. Depending on whether the visitor is an individual consumer or a business, the seller designs a marketing strategy that targets that particular segment. In general, both business and individual consumers will respond similarly to in changes in price, promotional offers, and in changes to the design of the webpage. The visitor segment drives how the seller designs the webpage, what products they offer, and what advertisements are used, and how their products are priced. The visitor segment can also be used to predict the behavior of individual visitors by predicting their needs and preferences.

PERSONALIZATION vs. CUSTOMIZATION

Personalization often overlaps with **Customization**, as the information is presented to consumers in a customized form. What a user might call customization might in fact be personalization or vice-versa. However, there are differences between customization and personalization. Customization is the process of configuring an interface and creating a profile manually by adding and removing elements in a profile. The user is actively involved in creating the look and the content of the webpages, and they have higher degree of control over it. Customization is mostly related to the resources, in terms of portal layout and webpages.

On the other hand, personalization is the process where users are passive and have a lower degree of control over the content and layout of the website. It is the sellers' websites which monitor, analyze and react to the behavior of users. Mass personalization is not generally possible for online sellers, the simple fact is that two customers are never completely alike. However, mass customization can also be accomplished, as has been shown in the previous example of Dell's website. All users have the ability to interact with the website and customize products to their own liking.

PERSONALIZATION vs. CUSTOMER RELATIONSHIP MARKETING

Many confuse personalization to **Customer Relationship Marketing** (CRM). But CRM and personalization are two different concepts in the marketing field. CRM deals with the relationship between the customer and the company. CRM helps to achieve high-level business goals, and personalization is a key component of CRM strategy. Personalization involves the work of many parties in the process of offering a product, and is the best way to increase customer-seller interaction and retain customers. Personalization requires the pooling of information from multiple sources, ranging from different department like finance, sales, and logistics to information directly gathered from the customer. CRM strategy also must take into account information about the external market, including market competitors, market trends, and an analysis of the industry.

Personalization is embedded in the core of the CRM strategy. It comes only after the data related to customers is collected and analyzed. Personalization helps to determine valued and existing customers and identifies potential customers that can be attracted with the right strategies, while recognizing which customers do not add any value to the company.

IMPORTANCE OF PERSONALIZATION

Personalization's importance comes from the one-to-one relationships where individual-specific profiles allow vendors to improve customer satisfaction. For example, if a customer already receives personalized shipping and gift recommendations on Staples. com, he will feel less inclined to switch to other online retailers and go through the same time-consuming process to receive the same recommendations. The customer is comfortable dealing with Staples because he has already availed himself of the personalized services. The personalized services given by the Staples webpage include, a complete listing of items that have been previously purchased, along with a list of items that are preferred by the user. In addition, they send a list of suggested products that a customer may be interested in based on his previous purchases. This helps to increase cross-selling possibilities, which in turn help to maintain loyalty and customer retention. Staples also sends email reminders for reordering the favorite item, or when there is a deal on a product that is found on the user's favorite list.

Business performance is affected by the level of personalized service offered by their website. There are different levels of personalization, starting with processes involved during customer interactions, which leads to the developing and analysis of customer profiles. Based on these levels of personalization, the company's website target their marketing activities towards the individual customer profile. The company then must find a way to charge fees to the customer for the personalized service that they offer. Some companies offer their specialized services through membership fees. Contactcenterworld.com[45] charges consumers a membership fee to access their collection of informative articles, case studies, interviews, analytical reports, and industry trends. The members can also submit questions to experts in relevant fields free of cost.

On the other hand, many companies, like Dell, offer customers the ability to customize products free of charge. When users register with a website, customized pages appear that are geared towards their needs and preferences. As these webpages are customized to meet the

---

45 This company was founded in 1999 by Raj Wadhwani to help operational managers and executives around the world to increase their knowledge and value through daily editorials and industry information. The website address www.contactcenterworld.com

demands of particular consumers, it is easier to offer promotions and discounts on particular products. These promotions and discounts generate more purchases from customers and helps to maintain a profitable relationship between the seller and the customer (Figure 1).

Figure 1: Screen shot of Dell PC.com

PERSONALIZED SERVICES

Personalized Services are offered in the form of personal webpages, recommended products, wish lists, e-mail notifications, and one-click technology. MyYahoo[46] is a good example of the provision of personalized services to its users. MyYahoo is a World-Wide-Web directory that was started by David File and Jerry Yang at Stanford University in 1994. Based on visitor sample profiles, it offers a wide variety of content coverage, including news, stocks, weather updates, greetings and purchases. In this webpage, the personalized service is offered in the form of a personal book. Personal book is an area on the website where the registered user can login and modify their personal

46 My Yahoo is a part of Yahoo.com. Yahoo! is a short form of *Yet Another Hierar-chical **O**fficious **O**racle. Its website is www.yahoo.com*

data. They can also access their personalized functions like wish lists and preferred content.

The content on Yahoo is based on the targeting of audiences which have been defined through research. Although this content is not an explicit example of a one-to-one relationship, it makes the user identify themselves with the group. Yahoo has made it possible for users to edit the content of the webpages that they viewed by changing the layout of their webpages to meet their preferences. This type of personalization is only possible through visitor segmentation.

Personalization is not limited to the selling of products. The benefits of personalization can also be experienced in the television and movie industries, in addition to industries dependent on the circulation of publications.

1. Personalization in the Entertainment Industry

The entertainment industry offers personalized services to strengthen and maintain its viewer segment. An example is the Canadian Broadcasting Center, CBC, which offers news, sports, entertainment, radio, and television listings of the Canadian entertainment industry. Once a viewer becomes a CBC member, they receive e-mail newsletters and alerts based on what they have indicated their preferences to be. Other features that make the website personal are areas where viewers can contribute comments to stories, submit reviews and rate articles, films, products, restaurants, and documentary. Users can also use the discussion forum to discuss issues and other topics. Another unique feature is the favorite member list, where users can keep a list of particular CBC member viewpoints and comments that they have an interest in. The list ensures that the user is alerted of any new contribution by the favorite members.

Following the examples of CBC TV, many companies in the television industry have started offering personalized services. Although these websites offer similar personalized services, the differentiation comes from the content layout and page presentation. The film industry has also started offering personalized services based on consumer preferences of actors, directors, or production agencies. This helps them to increase their customer base with respect to viewers and increases their overall earnings. In addition, additional personalized services increase consumer awareness of the movies being released. The user comments of other viewers are available online, giving potential viewers more information to decide whether or not they want to see a certain movie. Hollywood offers a website, www.hollywood.com, which offers trailers for movies that are soon to be released, celebrity news, fan clubs, and additional movie product offerings. The website also offers a personal book known as Myhollywood; where the viewers can list their favorite movies, rate and review any movie, connect with other viewers who have similar tastes in movies, and receive personalized news.

2. Personalization in Publication Industry

Personalization in the publication industry is important because it can bring people together based on their similar interests. Personalized services increase the awareness and thus increase the readership of the particular publication. The personalized services are offered in the form of articles, books, case studies and analytical reports. These services help to improve the knowledge of the readers. As these are very specialized services, the publisher generally charges a membership fee. For example, becoming a member of ACM provides unlimited access to online books, online courses, full-text articles from ACM's journals and magazines, and conference proceedings. The members can also access the career center, where they can view available jobs and apply for jobs in areas of their interest.

Some publications company offer free white papers or reports as a marketing strategy to attract new customers. 1 to 1 (www.1to1.com) is an excellent example for this type of personalized services offering. Backed by Peppers & Rogers Group[47], 1 to 1 provides print, electronic and custom publications to more than 250,000 decision makers and practitioners. They have a marketing strategy to attract new customers. When customers register with 1 to 1, , they get a free copy of the 1 to 1 white paper, "Building one-to-one Websites", in which they guide the customers through the process of developing their own websites.

TECHNOLOGIES

Information technology gathers information and serves the customer by anticipating their needs, makes the interaction satisfying and effective for both parties and builds a relationship for repeat purchases. Once the user's needs are established, the sellers can promote products that are useful to the user, even if the user is not currently aware of these products.

Personalization takes a set of well-defined inputs and makes product recommendations to users. The effectiveness of personalization is critically dependent on the ability of the vendor to extract information and the willingness of the customer to share information. The ability of the vendor to collect, store, process, and extract information is aided by the help of sophisticated technology. With the use of new technology,

---

47   A globally recognized leader in customer strategy and relationship marketing.

online vendors can collect information about point-of-sales, financial transaction information, and browsing activities. Best Buy[48], with the help of sophisticated technology, is able to design more accurate shopping profiles for each of its web customers. This has helped them gain a competitive edge in the Internet marketplace (Figure 2).

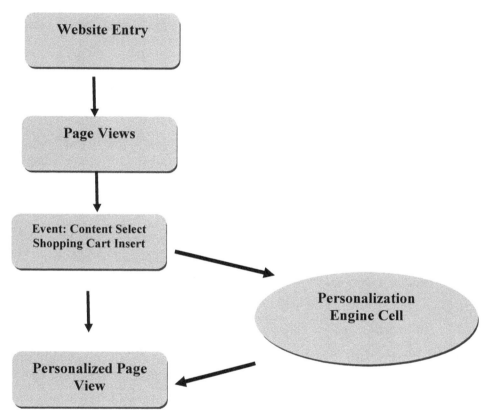

Figure 2: Typical Visitor Flow with a Personalization Engine Engaged

Successful companies are protective of the technology that gives them a competitive advantage. The **Personalization Engine** is

---

48   www.BestBuy.com is a online seller of consumer goods, electronics good, music, software etc.

integrated in their website to provide a personalized view of the webpage to web users. The personalization engine is a system where analytical models examine active users based on their past behavior. This enables the sellers to utilize the appropriate advertisement or promotion for their individual users at the right time. The personalization engine also provides more accurate forecasting tools, which is very useful in developing an effective personalization strategy.

A company's **Personalization Strategy** depends upon their business goals. Their personalization tools will generally be tailored to their overall business goals. The **User Interface Design** is an important part of the personalization process. When designing the user interface, the seller has to keep in mind that the goal is to create and maintain a long-term relationship with the customer. Therefore, the interface has to breed trust and comfort for the customer with respect to the business. The content and the navigation of the interface should be user friendly and easy so that the visitor fully understands the webpage and product offerings.

The interface is particularly useful in developing visitor profiles. There are two types of profiles: explicit and implicit. A distinct attribute for the **Explicit Profile** comes from customer responses. The **Implicit Profile** attributes come from watching customer behavior. The Explicit Profile uses technology like forms and online questionnaires whereas the Implicit Profile uses technology like cookies to develop the attributes. Other technologies that are used are Collaborative Filters and Click Stream Analysis for information gathering and analysis of inputs.

1. Neural Networks

Neural Networks are mathematical or computational models that are used to detect patterns in the data. It involves the use of fuzzy theory to identify patterns in real-time scenarios. Neural networks are very useful for performing segmentation of visitor profiles. However, it is not a very scalable technology. The models require a training period for businesses to be able to understand and evaluate patterns in the user activity. Based on these patterns, the seller will perform profile segmentation and forecasting of customer behavior. Once it "learns" the usual activity involved by the user, it has a difficult time to unlearn things. It is usually very tedious to unlearn in case of errors of judgment.

2. Collaborative Filtering

Collaborative Filtering is the process by which information or patterns are filtered through the collaboration of multiple agents, data sources and viewpoints. In personalization, collaborative filtering compares a user's tastes with those users who share similar tastes to forecast the behavior of customers with similar preferences. Amazon.com is an excellent example of where collaborative filtering is used to predict the behavior of a user based on its user population. For example, if a user buys item A, then, based on the behavior of other users who bought item A with item B, Amazon will suggest that its current user should buy item B as well. This type of suggestive selling can create interest for products the consumer did not initially have in mind but does have an interest in purchasing.

Collaborative filtering takes place in two stages. During the first stage, the users with the same rating patterns are compared with the active users and rated. In the second step, these ratings are used to forecast the behavior of the active users. The efficiency of this system depends on the size of the user population. The larger the user population, the more accurate the ratings will be and the higher the quality of the recommendation. As the quality of the recommendation is higher, customers will be more impressed and more likely to be repeat customers.

3. Forms

Forms are used by the seller to collect information about the user. Active involvement of the user is required for this technique to be effective. Forms allow customers to respond and show interest in the type of content and the look and feel of the user interface of the website. This technique requires the users to make extra effort to respond, thereby making the level of personalization dependent on the user's motivation to participate. If the users are not willing to spend time filling out forms and voicing their preferences, sellers cannot provide the highest level of service to their customers. In addition, if the users are not active with respect to providing updates of their preferences, the profile remains static and the sellers are unable to keep their personalization techniques current. Forms are used by the sellers wherever the customer is supposed to provide information. Forms are dependent upon the free will of the customer to share the information.

4. Click-stream Analysis

Click-stream is the process of collecting, analyzing, and reporting aggregate data about the pages a user visits. Click-stream is calculated by measuring the number of mouse clicks each user makes. It is considered to be the most effective technique of predicting and evaluating user behavior. Due to the fact that sellers handle large volumes of data, many of them prefer to use applications to help them interpret and generate reports on click-stream data.

There are two levels of click-stream analysis: traffic analysis and e-commerce analysis. In **Traffic Analysis**, the click stream data is collected by the server when a user navigates the website. It tracks the number of pages viewed by the user, the time spent on each webpage, and the number of hits on the "back" or "stop" button. Under **E-Commerce Analysis**, the click-stream data is used to determine the effectiveness of the site as a channel-to-market by calculating the user's behavior. It tracks the items user purchases, the flow of items in the shopping cart, and the pages where a user spends more time. The information collected can be used to segment and profile customers into applicable categories.

5. Expert Systems and Rule-based Engines

An **Expert System**, a very important system in artificial intelligence, uses knowledge to solve specific problems based on a series of questions. It initially involves the identification of user attributes and preferences. Then, rules are constructed based on these attributes. It is generally useful in online configuration, step-by-step help wizards and gift finders.

A rule-based engine uses a set of business rules to decide what content needs to be shown to the user and the different courses of action required. Rule-based engines are not dynamic and do not adjust to patterns over time. Rule-based engines are also difficult to maintain, because there is a great deal of complex coding involved in the maintenance process. Personalization is accomplished through the usage of the DB2 content Manager Runtime edition for storage of rules and other objects.

CONSUMER PRIVACY

Personalization is the foundation of e-marketing strategy and depends on the collection and use of personal information. Sellers handle a great deal of consumer information and data, and therefore must be very mindful of the privacy and security of consumers. Successful personalized services come from more detailed consumer information. Some personalization systems effectively balance personalization and privacy concerns. However, most systems do not manage this balance well. At the risk of providing superior personalized service to the consumer, the seller ultimately risks the privacy of the consumer. Although the sellers maintain, follow and address the privacy issue, there is still a concern as to whether online consumers are comfortable using personalized services.

To address the privacy concern, the Personalization Consortium was established. The **Personalization Consortium** is an international advocacy group that addresses the need for consumer privacy and security. It is based in USA, and its goals are to encourage the growth and success of electronic commerce through personalized electronic marketing. They develop, promote, and guide sellers involved in one-to-one marketing practices. The consortium includes Pricewaterhouse Coopers, American Airlines, and DoubleClick, and was established to provide ethical information and privacy management objectives. The work of the consortium better enables customers to confidently use personalization technology to their benefit without significant risks to the security of their information.

Consumer information scattered over different websites can give a very detailed profile of a consumer. As discussed in this chapter, the profiles are built using different information technology, helping companies to better personalize their products. Once the customer views these products, they visit the site where the products are located. Companies must ensure that the presentation of their product is attractive if they wish to attract more customers. The issues and challenges surrounding presentation are the focus of the next chapter, where it is seen that while personalization can bring the customer to the website, presentation of the product is what ultimately generates the sale of the product.

CASE STUDY

Amazon.com was founded as Cadabra.com in 1994 by Jeff Bezos in Seattle, Washington. In 1995, it was launched as Amazon.com. Amazon was one of the first companies to venture into e-commerce. They started out as only an online bookstore but, overtime, offer a wider range of products, including but not limited to computer software, apparel, furniture, pet food, video games, and CDs and DVDs. Amazon became successful because of its ability to provide products at lower price.

Amazon uses both their proprietary technologies and licensed technology to offer personalized services. They use forms to collect data of the customers. In addition, Amazon has established relationships with companies that specialize in search engines, database management and integration systems. They have used this technology to implement numerous features that enhance the customer's shopping experience. They also have technology that helps them perform more sophisticated data analysis.

Amazon (www.amazon.com)[49] illustrates the different aspects of personalization techniques in one-to-one marketing (Figure 3). It also illustrates the different features of personalized services. The customers are allowed to become registered users of its sites, free of charge. The data collected during the registration process allows Amazon.com to identify products of interest to its customers. The gathered information helps the sellers to create a Personal Book whenever the customer visits the website. A **Personal Book** has transaction history details, notification, and areas of interests. The company also provides wish lists that help to keep track of the customers' input about the products. This helps Amazon to recommend products to the customers or recommend websites that deal with the products of interests.

Another unique feature of the personalization techniques used by Amazon is the user rating of the products option. Customers can rate the products they buy on Amazon.com from 1 to 5, which provides information to other customers considering purchase of these products. Rating scales also provided a basic idea of the popularity and dependability of the product. The gift-giving recommendations help Amazon to collect information on people who are not their customers.

---

49 It *was launched in initially as Cadabra.com in 1994 by Jeff Bezos and its headquarters is located in Seattle, Washington. Started as an online bookstore, it is one of the first companies to venture into e-commerce and now offers wide range of products like DVDs, CDs, computer software, apparel, electronics, furniture, pet food, grocery, and video games.*

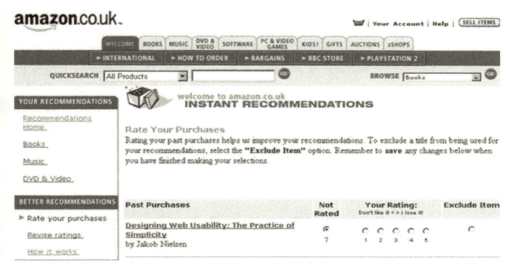

Figure 3: Screenshot of Amazon.com's Rating Facility

Other type of personalized services offered by Amazon are the Amazon.com Prime membership and One-click technology. Prime is a membership program that is used to provide faster delivery and more personalized services to their customers. A membership fee of $79 per year is charged, and the members receive free two-day shipping and discounted overnight shipping of $3.99 on all eligible items. One-Click Technology makes the purchasing process for customers faster by storing customer credit card information and delivery addresses. These features allow the sale to be processed much more quickly. Other examples of personalized services offered by Amazon.com are editorial reviews, product information, baby and wedding registries, customer channel preferences, and listings of new releases and top-sellers.

CHAPTER SUMMARY

Personalization refers to the practice of businesses individualizing marketing content and programs for customers based on their unique individual profiles. The aim of personalization is to improve the user's experience and create higher user satisfaction during their interactions with the website.

Many confuse personalization with customer relationship marketing (CRM). Personalization is a major component of CRM, which is an overall broader system of businesses managing their customers to achieve their overall business goals.

The different phases of personalization are customer interactions, customer profiles, analysis of profiles and customer data, and the targeting of marketing activities to suit the customer profile. Personalized services are offered in the form of personal webpages, recommendation areas, wish lists, e-mail notifications, and one-click technology. More user information can be obtained through any number of information technology techniques.

Personalization requires the use of different technology for information gathering and data analysis. The personalization engine is integrated in the company's website to provide individual customers a personalized view of the webpage. The user interface design is an important part of the design process. The user interface is particularly useful in developing visitor profiles. Personalization requires the use of neural networks, collaborative filtering, expert and rule based engines, forms, and clickstream analysis to build the profiles. Personalization of websites involve the gathering of detailed consumer information. This creates privacy concerns for customers. In response to these concerns, the Personalization Consortium was established, which has sought to limit the security risks customers incur by purchasing products online.

REVIEW QUESTIONS

1. In the 21st century, personalization has become the latest buzzword in Internet marketing strategy. Explain what personalization is and highlight its importance.

2. Organizations often have to choose between customization and personalization when developing a website. Explain the differences between customization and personalization and the relative benefits and disadvantages to the organization.

3. Customer Relationship Management has also become an important part of Internet marketing strategy. Is personalization an important concept to be considered when implementing this strategy?

4. What is personalized service? Explain, with examples, the personalized service that is offered in the film industry.

5. What are the technologies that are used to offer personalized services? Explain.

6. What is the role of the user interface when a designing a personal webpage?

7. What are visitor profiles and how are they developed?

8. How are the terms personalization and consumer privacy related? Explain them.

9. What is the Personalization Consortium?

REFERENCES

1. Aaronson, Jack (2007), *Personalization Technology: A Primer*; accessed on 18-3-2008; http://www.clickz.com/showPage. html?page=3626837

2. ACM; accessed on 24-3-2008; www.acm.org

3. Bonett, Monica (2001); *Personalization of Web Services: opportunities and Challenges*; Ariadne (28); http://www.ariadne. ac.uk/issue28/personalization/intro.html

4. CBC; accessed on 20-3-2008; http://www.cbc.ca/television/

5. D. Peppers, M. Rogers and B. Dorf, *"Is your company ready for one-to-one marketing?"*, Harvard Business Review (1999) 3–12.

6. *Enpocket; Personalization engine*; accessed on 21-3-2008; http://www.enpocket.com/solutions/enpocket%20platform/advanced-profiling-and-targeting

7. Harney, John (2003); *Personalization and CRM. Know thy customer.* Accessed on 23-3-2008; http://www.aiim.org/article-aiim.asp?ID=26712

8. Hollywood; accessed on 22-3-2008; www.hollywood.com

9. Jakob Nielsen's Alertbox for October 4, 1998: *Personalization is Over-Rated*
http://www.useit.com/alertbox/981004.html.

10. J. Alba, et al., *Interactive home shopping: Consumer, retailer, and manufacturer incentives to participate in electronic marketplaces*, Journal of Marketing 61 (1997) 38–53.

11. Lynch, C.A., *From Automation to Transformation*: Forty Years of Libraries and Information Technology in Higher Education, *Educause Review*, 35(1), January/February 2000, 60-68. http://www.educause.edu/pub/er/erm00/pp060068.pdf

12. Marketwire, 26 companies launch Consortium to promote responsible use of personalization technology; accessed on 12-

3-2008; http://findarticles.com/p/articles/mi_pwwi/is_200004/ai_mark01007798

13. Micheal Rosenberg, "*The personalization Story*"; ITworld; accessed on 11-3-2008; http://www.itworld.com/Man/2676/ITW010511rosenberg/

14. MyYahoo!; accessed on 11-3-2008; http://my.yahoo.com/?myHome

15. Personalization Consortium, accessed on 13-3-2008; http://www.personalization.org/personalization.html

16. PTV; accessed on 11-3-2008; http://www.ptv.ie/

17. Richi, Christian, Personalization is not a technology: Using web personalization to promote your business goal; accessed on 17-3-2008, http://www.boxesandarrows.com/view/personalization_is_not_technology_using_web_personalization_to_promote_your_business_goal

18. Riecken, D. (ed.) *Personalized Views of Personalization, Communications of the ACM*, 43 (8), August 2000, 27-28.

19. Rigby, Darrell K; Frederick F. Reichheld, Phil Schefter (2002). "*Avoid the four perils of CRM*". Harvard Business Review 80 (2):101-109.

20. Tebbe, M; Between the lines, InfoWorld Electronic, 20(16), 20 April 1998.

21. TechSpot (2006); *Customization vs. Personalization*; accessed on 15-3-2008; http://tech-munish.blogspot.com/2006/01/customization-vs-personalization.html

22. SIGIA-L mailing list archive; " *Cusatomize vs. Personalize*"; accessed on 12-3-2008; http://www.listquest.com/lq/search.html?ln=sigia

23. Smyth, B and Cotter, P., *A Personalized Television Listings Service, Communications of the ACM,* 43 (8), August 2000, 107-111.

24. Staples; accessed on 14-3-2008; www.staples.com

CHAPTER 10

PHYSICAL IMAGE

Chapter Contents

- Objectives
- Introduction
- Online Shopping
- The Process of Shopping Online
- Transforming the Physical Image Online
- Converting a Virtual Store Into an Effective Salesperson
- How to Keep a Virtual Store Entertaining
- Problems Encountered by Online Shoppers
- Measures to Improve Online Shopping
- Case Study: Online Shopping Experience on Starshop.com
- Chapter Review
- Review Questions
- References

OBJECTIVES

This chapter will introduce, define, and illustrate the importance of physical image. The expansion of marketing to include the Internet presents new challenges to marketers worldwide. This chapter focuses on customer bases, responding to buying patterns, opening and maintaining online stores, and transferring the physical image of products to the online format while maintaining brand strength. Marketers need to focus on enhancing customer shopping experience while making the shopping exercise convenient for web users.

The balance of replicating the shopping experience of a brick and mortar store online often creates a complex website which neither lives up to providing convenience nor a satisfactory shopping experience. On the other hand, online shoppers face several problems – locating products of their choice, problems related to the online shopping cart, obtaining information on products and accurate pricing. Marketers constantly need to devise ways to find out what products are sought. Websites need to provide sufficient information, in the form of text, pictures, and multimedia. Pricing information needs to be given well in advance of the final check out screen. Security while shopping online is another major concern for shoppers. Companies have to address this issue and build confidence of their online shoppers.

Despite the drawbacks, online shopping offers the advantages of purchasing at any time and from any location. Shoppers can choose products, compare them and obtain them at attractive prices. The case study of The Star Shop illustrates a successful use of several techniques, like mystery shopping, to ensure a favorable customer experience; thus helping them to have their fare share of loyal customers at their brick-and-mortar stores.

INTRODUCTION

As was discussed in the previous chapter, personalization strengthens the relationship with the customer. However, presentation of the product is what ultimately secures the sale.

Companies, while promoting their brands on the Internet, might fail to effectively differentiate their product from other brands. This may result in brands losing their appeal and market share. However, the Internet offers opportunities for marketers to be creative in differentiating their brands and brand delivery.

Despite the fact that companies have different motives in using the Internet, they all face the major challenge of maintaining their brand promises online. When companies fail to maintain their brand promise on the Internet, sooner or later they will face of the problem of erosion of brand strength. Eventually, erosion of brand strength leads to loss in market share. This chapter will highlight the importance of the physical image of the product to the appeal of the product to customers. This chapter will discuss how to create the physical image of a store and its products on the Internet. This chapter will also discuss the nuances of online shops, the types of products and services sold on the Internet, and the process of online shopping.

ONLINE SHOPPING

An **Online Shop** or **Virtual Store** is the replica of a brick-and-mortar store on the Internet. Online shops are also known as Internet shops, e-stores, e-shops or web-shops. Many top retailers like Gap Inc. and Best Buy have physical stores but have successfully created successful virtual stores. Companies need not necessarily have a physical presence to have a successful virtual store. For instance, www.ostrichesonline.

com only operates through a web-store, where they sell, ostrich flesh, eggs, feathers, and other ostrich related items. Another benefit of an online store is that it does not need to cater to B2C customers alone, because it can also be used for B2B transactions. Items that sell the most on the Internet (based on 2006 figures[50]), are apparel, accessories and footwear, followed by computer hardware and software. Automobiles, car parts, and home furnishings are also sold extensively on the Internet.

Virtual stores are used to sell both digital products, such as music, movies, software, and education, and tangible products through affiliate marketing. Certain categories of products have been more profitable online. Products that have a high value-to-weight ratio and those that have a market in remote locations have also been sold successfully on the Internet. Two successful types of products sold online are spare parts for electrical household goods and centrifugal pumps. Virtual stores are beneficial because retailers generally do not stock spare parts. Therefore, sourcing these products only when an order is placed through a web-store is more cost effective.

Products not suitable to be sold through a virtual store are those that have a low value-to-weight ratio, and products that need to be interacted with physically before being purchased. For example, items that need to be smelled, tasted, touched, or tried on may encounter more difficulty in online sales. However, some online retailers like Tesco and Gap Inc. have been successful in selling clothing and accessories.

It is not possible for all retailers to sell online. For this reason, some of the high-volume websites, like Amazon.com, and Yahoo! offer

---

50   "The State of Retailing Online 2007", www.shop.org, 2007

hosting services for smaller retailers. A collection of online stores is referred to as an **Online Marketplace** or **Virtual Shopping Mall**. Consumers have a wide array of products to choose from.

Shopping online offers several advantages. Customers can shop anytime during the day and from any location. Browsing through a wide range of products online is comparatively easier than walking through the aisles in a physical store and examining the products. Consumers with high-speed Internet connections can enjoy an enhanced shopping experience by browsing though content-rich websites and faster navigation in between webpages.

Online shopping offers several advantages to both customers and retailers. Online shopping can be significantly more convenient for customers, offering a broad range of products at competitive prices with sufficient product information. Companies benefit from a store that offers their products to customers 24/7 and the advantages derived from increased customer satisfaction.

However, there are several drawbacks to shopping on the Internet. Customers cannot inspect the items before purchase, which would otherwise happen in a physical store. Online retailers are at risk when purchases are made using stolen credit cards. Identity theft is another major concern, where customers' data is stolen from the retailer's website. Recently, "phishing" has emerged as a major problem faced by businesses online. Customers are fooled into giving personal information on a website that resembles a reputed company. This has led several retailers to generate a unique seal for each customer, which is placed on the company website. This provides customers with greater assurances that their personal information is not at risk of being stolen. Customers also need to be assured that the contact information provided to the retailer is not used for spam and telemarketing purposes.

THE PROCESS OF SHOPPING ONLINE

Typically, consumers visit an online store of their choice through a search engine. Once the customer reaches the website, the retailer allows the customer to pick items of his choice and place them in a virtual shopping cart. This is followed by a checkout process, where the customer inputs payment information and selects between various shipping and delivery options. Once the transaction is complete, the customer is generally notified about his purchase via e-mail.

Customers generally pay online with a credit card. There are several other online options of payment available, such as PayPal, Google Checkout, and U-GotCash. Other conventional methods of payment also exist, such as debit card, check, cash on delivery, wire transfer and postal money order. Some virtual stores do not allow shoppers from other countries or the usage of international credit cards. Other virtual stores accept these methods of payment and additionally allow customers to send gifts across the world.

TRANSFORMING THE PHYSICAL IMAGE ONLINE

Marketers must initially assess the current brand promise, with respect to the company's customers and competitors. Other factors, such as product attributes, style, durability, and service variables need to be analyzed. Marketers must understand what factors differentiate their brand from other brands. If product attributes are the selling point for the brand, this must be communicated to the customers. Using this as a platform, a story needs to be built to help the customers make better decisions. The importance of the distinguishing attributes must be clear to the customer. Therefore, the Internet plays a dual role in delivering the brand promise: 1) as an online salesperson and 2) by keeping the customer engaged and entertained through information-rich websites or through some form of entertainment.

CONVERTING A VIRTUAL STORE INTO AN EFFECTIVE SALESPERSON

One of the best ways to make a virtual store successful is for marketers to use the attributes of good salesperson and build websites based on them. So what are the attributes of a great salesperson? A great salesperson builds a trusting relationship with the customer and caters to the customer's needs and preferences. In addition, a great salesperson should be committed to the promises made by his business with respect to time, product quality, and performance. Finally, his emphasis should be on building long-term relationships with customers. The challenge for marketers is to replicate these attributes on the company's virtual store.

GE Lighting Systems has successfully differentiated its brands on its website (Exhibit I). When it came to effectively using all of the attributes of salesmanship on its website, GE Lighting Systems missed the mark. The company lacked integrating in the eyes of its customers. On the other hand, Otis Elevator used its website to interact with its customers. It used its website to monitor its product performance in the remote facilities of its customers. Otis Elevator offered advice and helped with maintenance and repair of its product. The after-sales integration gave the company an insight into its products, the usage patterns of its products, and other valuable customer information.

GE's Approach to Brand Differentiation

General Electric has a wide portfolio of businesses. One of their decisions, GE Lighting Systems offers several products, the most prominent being light bulbs. Since bulbs, from the customer's point of view, are almost the same irrespective of its brand name, there is little scope for brand differentiation. Differentiating the brands becomes a daunting task especially on the Internet. However, GE differentiated with respect to its competitors by focusing on the broad range offered. Further, it engages the customers by inviting them to develop lighting solutions for their properties and allows them to view the effect of these combinations. This helped GE to focus on solutions rather than products alone. It also gave GE an opportunity to build interactive relationships and understand customers' requirements.

"We'll take you to the right lamp, even if you don't know what you need" – This is the slogan on the GE website. It reflects the company's focus on understanding the customer's need and solving the problem. The site has employed enough tools to let the customer explore the portfolio of GE Lighting Systems. However, sales are not online. The website acts more as a promotional site rather closing deals online.

Exhibit I: GE's Approach to Brand Differentiation

Source: Rob Lachanauer, David E Williams, Matthias Becker, "How the Internet Boost Your Brand", E-Marketing – The Emerging Trends, Icfai University Press, 2006

HOW TO KEEP A VIRTUAL STORE ENTERTAINING

Effective salesmanship also involves the use of entertainment. Virtual stores can use entertainment to establish connections with customers and obtain valuable information about the customers.

There are instances where companies manufacturing industrial machinery have used entertainment to keep the customer interested in their product offerings. For example, the Fisher-Rosemount division of Emerson, which provides highly flexible, open-system architecture for plant automation, offers an entertaining, game-like simulation of the SimCity series of games on its website. Visitors to the website can use tools to build different plant configurations. This game provides customers with an understanding of the technical benefits of the Fisher-Rosemount products and the potential savings for each plant configuration. The company also gains tremendous insight into the visitors' needs.

Another company that used entertainment on its website is Timberjack, a supplier of forestry gear. On its website, it offered its customers video product galleries, merchandise promotions and information about sponsored leisure events. Along the same lines, General Electric included an online game in which the registered users could access and win cash prizes. This gave customers the opportunity to learn about GE products.

PROBLEMS ENCOUNTERED BY ONLINE SHOPPERS

Several industry observers have observed that virtual stores are a complex environment. Purchasing decisions are driven by the consumer's level of involvement and engagement in the online experience. Therefore, as customers are looking at the Internet for their shopping needs, marketers need to constantly devise methods to create enjoyable shopping experiences similar to what customers experience while shopping in malls and other brick-and-mortar stores.

Research has shown that certain features of the online interface have a direct influence on customer purchasing decisions. These features can influence the frequency of purchases and also contribute to impulsive purchases. However, simply adding features to the online store is not sufficient to influence impulsive purchases. Customers must be exposed to the entertainment features on the online store, which will contribute to impulsive purchases. Web features that influence shoppers to experiment and shop by exploring have the maximum influence on impulsive buying.

Technology has improved to such an extent that a retailer on his online store can help shoppers simulate the experience of trying on a dress, accessories and other items, thus enhancing the experience for the shopper. Companies must continue to use research tools, such as online newsletters and forms, to gather information about the long-term intentions of buyers and their willingness to continue to shop online.

Internet shopping research has shown that the acceptable website response time is about 4 seconds. If a website takes more than 4 seconds to respond, it is highly probable that the customer might lose interest and move to a different website. This indicates that the online customer is highly demanding. While web retailers are looking for the best way to produce a shopping experience that will increase sales, web shoppers are looking for virtual stores that are fast and always available.

So, how can web retailers gain an insight into the shopper's online behavior and expectations? Certain metrics, such as page views and surf time provide some information. On average, the online visitor spends more than eight minutes and 18 page views before making a purchase. In addition, a simple task like checking the validity of a gift certificate, on average, takes two minutes and five page views. This evidence is contrary to the claim that online shopping saves consumers time.

The normal focus of marketers and researchers is the design features of a company's website. However, online shoppers face significant problems outside of the issue of the design of the website. For example, shoppers frequently encounter problems with several page views, checkout, sufficient product information, price, and shipping costs. Online shoppers also face the problem of locating their preferred goods and services on the website. These problems, when encountered regularly, lead to customer dissatisfaction.

Another major problem encountered by online shoppers pertains to the shopping cart feature. Many online shoppers have difficulty locating the shopping cart while they are on the website. In addition, shoppers find it difficult to add items to their shopping cart. Even if the items are loaded in the shopping cart, the most common complaint is the delay in getting the information about the total cost of the products in the cart. Furthermore, on most shopping sites, the checkout process is the only way to get information about pricing, taxes, and shipping and handling charges. Sometimes shoppers have to wait to obtain this information, or they are forced to register for a catalog or provide personal information before they can find out the total amount to be paid. Research has shown that shoppers will abandon their shopping carts at the checkout due to the inconveniences associated with the process. Therefore, online stores must present and provide total price information prior to the checkout. Retailers must realize that online shoppers are sensitive to prices and must have all stages of the shopping process be convenient to follow through with the purchase.

MEASURES TO IMPROVE ONLINE SHOPPING

There is no doubt that companies selling online understand the significance of the shopping experience to the customers. However, many falter when they try to duplicate the offline shopping experience virtually. There are methods outside of simple duplication of in-person shopping that companies can focus on to improve their online stores.

It is essential that online retailers present their products in a way that makes it easy for shoppers to locate items of their choice. They must understand customer preferences, which can be monitored by tracking sales information, traffic within the site and by monitoring the keywords used in search engines.

When online shopping became popular, there was a concern that consumers may be given too much information on websites. However, online shopping can only be enriched by providing information that a customer might not receive in physical stores. For instance, the online shopper benefits from receiving additional product information, comparative products and services, alternatives to the product or service, and the attributes of each alternative.

Online retailers must describe their products creatively by using text, pictures and animation. It is important to provide, to the extent possible, an experience of demonstration or 'trying out' of the product so that the customers do not feel they are missing out by shopping online instead of in a physical store. Apart from basic information, shoppers need to be informed about the instructions of use, safety procedures and manufacturer specifications. To further increase customer engagement and gain an insight into the customer's purchasing intentions, certain online stores allow customers to rate their products and services. Creative gathering of information on a website can only help marketing the products.

Research suggests that the complexity and novelty of information needs to be maintained on a web-store. **Complexity** refers to the various elements or features of a website resulting from increased diversity of information. Novelty of information leads to consumers further exploring the website and making more impulsive purchases.

Studies have also revealed that female shoppers are more interested in a superior web experience rather than male shoppers. This is also true when men and women shop in physical stores. Female shoppers are more likely to compare prices and products. Therefore, a company's website must include features that allow shoppers to view pictures of the product and rotate images, similar to how they would inspect a product in a physical store.

Even though companies should look to fix shopping cart and other presentation problems, more emphasis needs to be on problems related to website hierarchy, navigation and search. Furthermore, companies must make the information customers look for available and highly visible, especially related to pricing, taxes, and shipping charges. It is also important that retailers note the number of page views in the purchasing process and the loading time. As these two numbers increase, the satisfaction of shopping online decreases. To create more favorable shopping experiences and generate sales, online retailers must build technologically advanced websites with faster loading times, effective search features, and insightful features of the virtual store (Exhibit II).

Research Insights on Online Customer Experiences

Elliott and Fowell conducted research on the shopping experience of online customers. The findings are listed below.

Satisfactory Experiences:

- Convenient to shop anytime and from anywhere
- Lower prices can be expected
- Customized shopping experience
- Instant delivery of digital products and services

Unsatisfactory Experiences:

- Product promised and product delivered were not the same
- Poor service
- Higher prices charged
- Difficulty in using the virtual store
  Security concerns

Exhibit II: Research Insights on Online Customer Experiences

Source: Steve Elliot and Sue Fowell, "Expectations versus reality: a snapshot of consumer experiences with Internet retailing", International Journal of Information Management, 2000

Companies face the challenge of transferring the physical image of the product into brand strength. However, special attention is required to follow existing protocol in conducting online transactions. As transactions are carried out in different countries, companies must follow the business protocol of those countries. Therefore, protocol has become an incredibly important consideration that is now a component of the e-marketing mix. The next chapter will discuss the importance of protocol and how it changes the behavior of e-enabled organizations.

CASE STUDY

ONLINE SHOPPING EXPERIENCE ON STARSHOP.COM*

Star Shop is one of the largest retailers in the USA. The company, established during the late 1970s, has grown from a small grocery chain of 5 stores to a multi-product chain of more than 200 stores across the country. Star Shop was known for their focus on customers and provision of great customer service. They used several techniques, like mystery shopping, to create a favorable customer experience. This led to Star Shop gaining a good number of loyal customers to their brick-and-mortar stores.

Upon the realization that its customers spent a significant amount of time shopping online, Star Shop installed a virtual store. It used its data bank of email lists to mail catalogs to customers and directed them to the virtual store. Over a period of time, the customer service division received a number of letters from disgruntled and angry shoppers. The head of the division, Amanda Garett, was puzzled with the number of angry letters. She decided to shop on the Star Shop web-store herself to find out what exactly was wrong.

The following weekend, Amanda opened her mailbox to find the latest catalog of StarShop.com among her e-mails. When she reached the website, she observed that there were 17 pages of products for customers to view. Amanda wondered whether a customer would see all the 17 pages. She started to choose items of interest and added them to her shopping cart, and continued to shop by clicking on 'Keep Shopping'.

On subsequent pages, whenever Amanda selected an item it took her to a page that displayed the message, 'Sorry, this item is no longer available'. Amanda wondered why items that were unavailable were not removed from the online store.

She continued further and selected another item for her cart. Immediately, a message popped up to show that all of the items she had previously selected were no longer in her shopping cart. Amanda now realized why so many customers were frustrated and understood that there must be something wrong with shopping cart software that was used. She sent an e-mail to Customer Service, like any other shopper, and shared her experience and dissatisfaction. A couple of hours later, she received the following e-mail, which seemed familiar, from the Customer Service at StarShop.com:

> *Dear Ms. Amanda,*
> *Thank you for contacting us. It is wonderful to hear from you! We are happy to receive your mail. The mail has been forwarded to the appropriate department for review.*
>
> *If you have any other queries, please visit our website www. StarShop.com or call us at 1-800-782-7467.*
>
> *We appreciate the time you have taken to write to us. We look forward to serving you in the future.*
>
> *Regards,*
> *Amanda,*
> *Customer Service*
> *StarShop.com*

Amanda knew that this was an automatically generated e-mail sent from her e-mail address. She realized that the e-mail was cordial but it never addressed the problem she had shared in her e-mail. She immediately decided to make a formal report to the head of the online store at Star Shop.

Source: "Where did my dress go?"
http://customersrock.wordpress.com/2007/01/29/where-did-my-dress-go/

*This case study is based on a fictional company. Any resemblance to the name is purely coincidental. The case study is based on the experience of an online shopper which was posted on a blog.

CHAPTER SUMMARY

The 1990s have witnessed a major shift towards online shopping in both developed and developing countries. This trend creates new challenges for businesses across the world. Many businesses are forced to establish stores online to maintain and expand their customer base. Once web-stores are established, businesses face yet another challenge – transferring the physical image of the product and the brand strength to the virtual store. Marketers must also focus on enhancing the shopping experience and making the process convenient for customers. In an attempt to replicate the shopping experience of a store, companies end up creating complex websites that do not provide convenient or enjoyable shopping experiences.

Although online shopping has been very beneficial to customers, online shoppers still face several problems: locating products of their choice, problems related to the shopping cart feature, and obtaining information on products and pricing. Marketers constantly need to devise ways to find out what products are in the highest demand. In addition, the company's website must provide sufficient information in the form of text, pictures, and multimedia. Pricing information needs to be given well in advance, not only at the time of checkout. Another major concern for online shoppers is security of personal information. Companies must address this issue and build the confidence of online shoppers so that they are willing to continue to shop online.

Despite its drawbacks, online shopping offers the advantage of purchasing at any time and from any location. Shoppers can choose products, compare them, and obtain at attractive prices in a matter of seconds. Several retailers have successfully provided an enhanced shopping experience while still making the process convenient for customers. To maintain and attract more customers, companies must monitor online shopping behavior and respond accordingly with the best website-user interface and other features.

REVIEW QUESTIONS

1. How can a company differentiate its brands online? Visit the website of Dell Inc. and examine how it differentiates its brands.

2. Should a retailer try to completely replicate a physical store online? Explain

3. Explain the problems faced by an online shopper.

4. How can online shopping be improved? Should a company focus on shopping experience or convenience? Discuss.

5. With respect to the case study, what were the problems faced by Amanda?

6. How should StarShop.com respond to Amanda's problems?

7. What should StarShop.com do to improve customer satisfaction? Explain.

REFERENCES

1. Rob Lachanauer, David E Williams, Matthias Becker, "*How the Internet Boost Your Brand*", *E-Marketing – The Emerging Trends*, Icfai University Press, 2006

2. Robert Strenge, "*WSU Researchers Explore Consumers' Online Buying Behavior*", http://researchnews.wsu.edu/society/130.html

3. S.L. Jarvenpaa & P.A. Todd, "*Consumer reactions to electronic shopping on the world wide web*", *International Journal of Electronic Commerce*, 1997

4. "*Best Practices Can Improve E-Commerce Experience*", http://www.ecommercetimes.com/story/38972.html, 2004

5. R.A. Peterson, S. Balasubramanian & B.J. Bronnenberg, "*Exploring the implications of the Internet for consumer marketing*", *Journal of the Academy of Marketing Science*, 1997

6. "*Creating the Ultimate Online Shopping Experience: User Behavior and Purchase Decisions in E-Commerce*", http://www.nycupa.org/pastevent_05_0126.html

7. "*K-State Marketing professor studies online shopping experience*", http://www.innovations-report.com/html/reports/studies/report-56426.html

8. "*Virtual Stores*", http://www.allprofitallfree.com/v-stores.html

9. Stephen F. King en Juhn-Shiuan Liou, "*A framework for internet channel evaluation*", International Journal of Information & Management, 2004

10. "Where did my dress go?", http://customersrock.wordpress.com/2007/01/29/where-did-my-dress-go/

11. M. Huang, *"Information load: its relationship to online exploratory and shopping behavior"*, 2000

12. *"The State of Retailing Online 2007"*, Shop.org Research, 2007

13. Steve Elliot and Sue Fowell, *"Expectations versus reality: a snapshot of consumer experiences with Internet retailing"*, *International Journal of Information Management* , 2000

CHAPTER 11

PROTOCOL

Chapter Contents

- Objectives
- Introduction
- Definition of Protocol
- Systems and Procedures
- Internationalization and Localization
- Culture
- Legal and Ethical Issues
- Other Issues of Concern
- Case Study
- Chapter Summary
- Review Questions

OBJECTIVES

The objective of this chapter is to discuss the importance of Protocol, which is one of the important Ps of the Contemporary Marketing Mix. This chapter will discuss the meaning of protocol and how it is necessary to maintain strong policies when it comes to online transactions. This chapter will discuss the requirements of Systems and Procedures in digital organizations. Furthermore, this chapter presents an example of an organization's protocol on its website, and how this benefits both the company and its customers. The importance of Internationalization, Localization, and Culture will also be discussed.

This chapter will provide insight into the ethical and legal issues involved in Internet business and the usage of technology. This chapter also evaluates how a company must protect itself and how companies can enhance their image in the marketplace by following appropriate protocols. The chapter ends with a case study which discusses a B2C organization based in Norwalk, Connecticut, and its commercial website that helps consumers get discounted tickets, hotel stays, and other travel related merchandise.

INTRODUCTION

Businesses are affected by the dynamics of the marketplace in a number of ways. The previous chapter discussed how the presentation of the products on a website can help businesses attract more customers and experience growth and profitability. Although the content of the company's website may help to increase the sales in one country, the same content may create legal issues in other countries, making sales difficult. Therefore, Hence, businesses must be aware of the existing **Protocols** and guidelines for conducting business in different countries.

This chapter will demonstrate how adherence to protocol enables e-businesses to attract more consumers.

Most companies have important roles in society, because they provide consumers with demanded goods, provide jobs, and generate tax revenue for the government, allowing the government to provide additional services for its constituents. In this intricate and interdependent marketplace, businesses with integrated digital technology and an Internet presence must be aware of Business Protocol. Business Protocol consists of the systems, procedures, and ethical, legal, and compliance issues relating to e-commerce. New technology (for example, gadgets like cell phones[51] used to send wireless web mails) is affecting more lives than ever before. E-Business regulatory issues, along with other issues concerning security and privacy, are becoming more important. These considerations require businesses to follow protocol carefully to manage the competing interests of consumers and regulatory influences.

When a company creates a website, it can be accessed from an Internet connection in any country. Companies have little to no control over where their website is accessed from. Companies that intend to attract customers from different countries must also understand that they must comply with the business rules and regulations of these different countries. Establishing an Internet presence means that e-businesses become part of the global marketplace. These e-businesses become subject to the laws of every state and country in which they have presence. Business regulations vary greatly from country to country. In addition, cultural and political differences also make things complicated for e-businesses looking to market their products

---

51 http://pwebs.net/marketing/ethics/articles/internetethics.htm

globally. Furthermore, companies must be prepared to market their products and their website in different languages to meet the demands of customers from different countries. Successful e-businesses are sensitive to these considerations and follow the appropriate protocol in the markets where they are actively involved.

DEFINITION OF PROTOCOL

Protocol is a code of conduct[52] or a set of guidelines or rules that organizations follow to achieve their objectives. A protocol is a set of rules that governs the communications between the electronic devices[53] or the computing endpoints. Company websites are accessed by people from different countries, making compliance with pricing policy, taxes, and other business regulations difficult. The creation of a website in an international domain is even a complex process. For example, Ikea, when entering a Canadian marketplace, must have a different domain name than its domain name in an Italian market. Companies entering the Internet marketplace must have certain standards and operating procedures that will protect them from legal liability, along with the preparation to meet the demands of customers of different countries.

SYSTEMS AND PROCEDURES

E-Commerce technology allows for better communication, coordination, and information interpretation. E-Commerce offers efficient technology solutions[54] that eliminate the need for traditional business processes, while the overall sales and product offering process becomes faster. In the Internet marketplace, competition is generally more intense than traditional markets, because there is no limit to the

---

52 http://vocabulary-vocabulary.com/dictionary/protocol.php
53 http://www.answers.com/topic/protocol?cat=health
54 Electronic Commerce 2008, Efraim Turban, Jae Kyu Lee, Dave King, Judy McKay, Peter Marshall, Prentice Hall, 5th Edition; 2008

availability of information about any product. Furthermore, the search costs for customers are lower, with the increased ability to compare different products instantly. The Internet marketplace provides customers the option of personalizing their products at lower prices with enhanced customer services. When dealing with this advanced technology, businesses require proper systems and procedures so that managers can effectively plan and organize their business activities[55].

Each company establishes a set of appropriate communication formats for their written correspondence, such as letters, memorandums, and business reports. Adequate consideration must be given to the design and use of office forms, composition of messages, proofreading and editing of all documents, and word processing. Businesses must also exercise care with respect to oral and non-verbal communication. Businesses should establish standard employee procedures for handling telephone calls, scheduling appointments, receiving visitors, mail management (incoming/outgoing), records management, and other related activities like business travel, meetings, conferences, training, and financial activities. For example, Web Results Inc.[56] deals with interactive design and web hosting. Web Results Inc. has designed its own protocol for its products and services to protect itself, its customers, and the Internet community in general from irresponsible and illegal activities. An example of the use of protocol is Web Results Inc.'s disclaimer, shown below in Exhibit I.

---

55 Systems and procedures for Modern Office: A simulation approach; Judith C Simon, Lillian H Chaney, Prentice Hall

56 http://www.webresultsinc.com/acceptableuse.htm. Web Results, Inc. is an organization started in 1998 dealing in interactive design and web hosting with specialization in providing solutions for web, print and multimedia. WRIs areas of expertise include CD & DVD development, web programming, graphic design, marketing consulting and multimedia strategies.

Prohibited Uses of WRI's Products and Services

Content: Web Results Inc. cannot be held responsible for the content of pages hosted under our service. WRI does not review pages for content before they are posted and does not verify, endorse, or otherwise take responsibility for the content of any user-created pages. However, we reserve the right to remove any page from our servers, which we determine is violating our rules and guidelines. Users are solely responsible for all files contained in their own directory, and can be held legally liable for the contents of their website.

Transmission, distribution or storage of any material in violation of any applicable law or regulation is prohibited. This includes, without limitation, material protected by copyright, trademark, trade secret or other intellectual property right used without proper authorization, and material that is obscene, adult, and defamatory, constitutes an illegal threat, or violates export control laws.

Network Usage: Knowingly engage in any activities that will cause a denial-of-service (e.g., synchronized number sequence attacks) to any WRI customers or end-users whether on the WRI network or on another provider's network. Using WRI's Services to interfere with the use of the WRI network by other customers or authorized users. The WRI network may be used by the Customer to link into other networks worldwide and the Customer agrees to conform to the acceptable use policies of these networks. In addition the Customer undertakes to conform to the Internet protocols and standards. The customer may not circumvent user authentication or security of any host, network, or account (referred to as "cracking" or "hacking"), nor interfere with service to any user, host, or network (referred to as "denial of service attacks"). Without prejudice to the foregoing, WRI considers that any application that overloads the network by whatever means will be considered as making profligate use of the network and is as such NOT allowed. Use of IP multicast other than by means provided and coordinated by WRI is likewise prohibited. Customers who violate systems or network security may incur criminal or civil liability. WRI will fully cooperate with investigations of suspected criminal violations, violation of systems or network security under the leadership of law enforcement authorities. Obtaining or attempting to obtain service by any means or device with intent to avoid payment. Unauthorized access, alteration, destruction, or any attempt thereof, of any information of any WRI customers or end-users by any means or device.

Electronic Communication: Customers are forbidden to send e-mail to any person who does not wish to receive it (non opt-in). It is explicitly prohibited to send unsolicited bulk mail messages ("junk mail" or "spam") of any kind (commercial advertising, political tracts, announcements,...) or to post the same or similar messages to large numbers of newsgroups (excessive cross-posting or multiple-posting, also known as "USENET spam"). Unauthorized use, or forging, of mail header information (e.g. "spoofing"). Customers may not forward or propagate chain letters, nor malicious e-mail. These rules apply to any Internet based distribution medium and any application using the Internet as well (for example, Usenet News, fax-like documents over the Internet). A customer may not solicit mail for any other address other than that of the customer, except with full consent of the owner of the referred address. Advertising, transmitting, or otherwise making available any software, program, product, or service that is designed to violate this AUP, which includes, but is not limited to, the facilitation of the means to send e-mail spam, initiation of pinging, flooding, mailbombing, denial of service attacks, and piracy of software. Sending email designed to damage the target system when executed or opened; for example, sending malicious programs or viruses attached to an email. Sending email which is designed to cause confusion, consternation, fear, uncertainty, or doubt, such as fake virus warnings. You must never subscribe anyone other than yourself to a mailing list. Maintaining an open mail (SMTP) relay.

Exhibit I: Disclaimer of WRI

Source: www.wri.com

INTERNATIONALIZATION AND LOCALIZATION

Businesses are globalized in two stages: Internationalization and Localization. **Internationalization** is the process by which the software used by an e-business is processed to accept foreign languages, foreign currencies, date formats, and other country-specific variations involved in conducting a business globally. **Localization** is the process by which translations and cultural adaptations of a website's content are performed.

An example of internationalization and localization comes from Oracle. Oracle's website, accessed in China, has its database and webpages encoded in 16-bit characters to handle the Chinese languages. In this way, Oracle's business recognizes the necessity for Internationalization. The software used by e-businesses should be compatible with Unicode[57] and other computing software standards to ensure worldwide access to their products and services through their websites. Internationalization requires an emphasis on the presentation of the webpages in a way that will be acceptable to the different

---

57 www.unicode.org

countries and cultures that will potentially view the webpage. There are various translation websites, like www.freetranslation.com, which provide free translation for software and other content. Exhibit II provides an example of another translation site, www.BabelFish.com, hosted by yahoo.com, where translations are performed easily. However, e-businesses must recognize that these machine translations are not 100 percent accurate, and the help of a human translator is required for complete accuracy. The advantage of using a human translator over a machine comes from the human understanding of cultural variations, market terminology, and other regional issues.

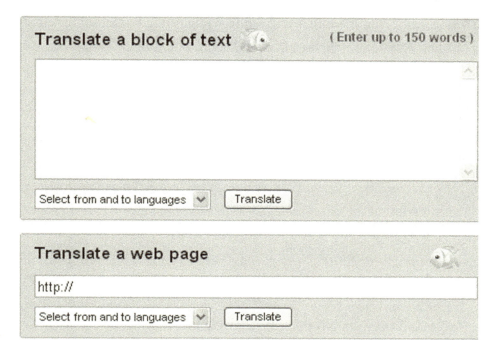

Exhibit II: Translation Services Provided on Yahoo.com
Source: http://babelfish.yahoo.com/

Localization refers to the layout and design of a website for the purpose of accommodating the foreign text. The most popular language for website presentation is English, and most e-business websites are designed to fit English. However, languages like Persian, Arabic,

Hebrew or Japanese that are read from right to left, instead of left to right, have to be presented in a different layout. The font size of the text is also affected when the language changes, affecting the readability. In addition, localization addresses the cultural associations of colors in different parts of the world. Color perception is very important to customers' opinions on all forms of advertising. Consequently, a website's use of colors has the potential to affect the purchasing decisions made by the visitors. The most acceptable color, across different cultures, is blue. Most of the e-businesses stick to the use of blue on their websites. Apart from color, it is very important to maintain neutral content that is accepted all over the world. For example, promoting beef products in the Indian e-marketplace will not be a successful plan for e-grocery stores targeting East Indian customers, because the religious beliefs of East Indians prohibits them from eating beef.

The most important aspect of Localization is presenting the content in a way that is understood by the local market. Keeping local markets and customers in mind is important in the presentation of all content, even pricing information. The prices must be displayed in the local currency or the exchange rate information should be provided such that customers in different countries will readily understand the cost of the product or service being offered. The website's content must effectively present information to the global, regional, and local markets. **Global Content** refers to general information that is the same for people of all countries, such as logos, trademarks, the company's history, and mission statement. **Regional Content** is adapted to suit the regional marketplace and includes information on products and promotions specific to a region. **Local Content** has information like delivery agencies, pricing, and office locations specific to a locality.

CULTURE

As websites are accessed by users of different cultures, different marketing approaches are required by e-businesses. E-Businesses must adapt their marketing strategies to suit the different cultures of their potential customers. Cultural differences can manifest themselves in the preference of consumers' payment methods, ease of accessibility and availability of the Internet, and cost of Internet access. For example, the consumers in the United States prefer to use credit cards to pay for their online purchases, but consumers from Asia prefer offline payments like checks or payment on delivery of the merchandise.

Cultural differences are additionally seen in the way the consumers are addressed. For example, European and Asian consumers prefer formality, whereas consumers in the United States prefer informality. As mentioned previously, the font type, the language, and the style of the website's content are all aspects of the cultural issues that must be considered when establishing an e-business.

The national culture affects the performance of an e-business in a country. The accessibility to e-businesses is different for each region. North America ranks the highest in e-business readiness, followed by Europe[58]. The readiness for e-businesses is affected by the political stability, taxation policy, and economic strength of a country. The other factors that contribute towards e-business readiness and performance are the literacy rates of the area's consumers, computer proficiency, the affordability of computers and Internet services, and the availability of good infrastructure. Without widely available Internet access, an e-business will have a difficult time succeeding.

---

58   Source: *2005 e-readiness rankings*, Economist Intelligence Unit

CHAPTER 11

LEGAL AND ETHICAL ISSUES

Laws are created for broad purposes and are intended to govern the conduct of national and sometimes international populations. Ethics is the study of non-legal moral norms that take into account the concerns and values of a society as a whole. The central focus of ethics lies in differentiating between right and wrong actions.

Although there is a relationship between ethics and legality, they are separate entities. Ethical codes historically have been established by groups of individuals who have special skills or knowledge. There are different views with respect to the role of law and self-regulation in the promotion of ethical online behavior. Some of the critical issues in the Internet business environment, with respect to legal and ethical issues include:

- The intellectual property -- who owns intangible property or technology
- Privacy -- privacy of the individual's identity and personal information, along with control of access to the e-business's website
- Extent of freedom of expression -- establishing the limit of freedom of expression when e-businesses are presenting content on their websites
- Data collection methods and how business ultimately use that data
- The status of children who log into digital networks with respect to e-business marketing strategy

In addition to the above mentioned issues, there are many obstacles to implementing e-businesses in the global environment. To address the legal and cultural challenges of globalization, taxation, distribution of products, and payment in the global economy, all e-businesses should follow the Global Standardization Protocol formed by the UNCEAFCT and OASIS.

The United Nations Center for Trade Facilitation and Electronic Business (UNCEFACT)[59] , a subsidiary of the United Nations Economic Commission for Europe, is a part of United Nations. The UNCEFACT oversees the business standards and practices among e-businesses. It encourages close collaboration between governments and private organizations while overseeing the inter-operability processes among them to encourage a secure and hassle-free form of trade.

Another non-profit consortium that drives the adoption of open standards in e-business is the Organization for the Advancement of Structured Information Standards (OASIS)[60]. OASIS was started in 1993 under the banner of Standard Generalized Markup Language (SGML). The SGML overlooked the development of standards and guidelines for inter-operability among products that support the SGML. OASIS also developed guidelines for Extensible Markup Language (XML) and other web service standards. The SGML has more than 5,000 participants representing over 600 organizations in over 100 countries. OASIS is a non–profit organization that has become popular due to its transparent governance and operating procedures that support e-businesses.

---

59 http://www.unece.org/cefact/about.htm
60 http://www.oasis-open.org/who/

UNCEFACT and OASIS, in 1999, started ebXML to deliver specifications and standards on the use of XML for business processes, registries and repositories, messaging, collaboration protocol agreements, and core data components. This technology allowed organizations of any size, located in any place, to conduct business over the Internet. They created and developed technical specifications for the open ebXML infrastructures. With the help of ebXML, companies now have a standard method available to exchange business messages, trading relationships, communicate data in common terms, and define and register business processes.

OTHER ISSUES OF CONCERN

Some other areas of concern include companies following the wrong procedures during copywriting and publishing for clients, un-researched articles about people and organizations that portray them negatively, and inaccurate blogs that can reflect badly on websites from the perspective of potential customers. Even e-mail correspondence (especially e-mail marketing) should be private and confidential without quoting from other sources, unless consent is given by the respective authors. Other ethical issues that must be considered in the presentation for any website include copyright infringement issues, credit/cash policies, trading at the international level, tariffs, website offers, privacy, consumers survey scams and hoaxes, advertising and keyword scams through spyware and adware programs, identity theft and Internet frauds, phishing, and domain name registration issues.

This chapter has discussed the different ethical concerns that arise when the company does not follow protocol. Unless an organization has standard ethical and legal guidelines, or there are active regulatory agencies protecting individuals, ethical and legal concerns have the potential to spiral out of control. Without control over these concerns, Internet business is not likely to be successful. The privacy issue has become one of the most discussed issues in e-commerce. The next chapter will explain the importance of securing the privacy of the customers during the online shopping process.

CASE STUDY

Priceline.com is an online travel services provider based in Norwalk, Connecticut. Priceline.com is a commercial website designed to help consumers get discounted prices on airline tickets, hotel rooms, and other travel related items. Priceline operates more than one website, including travelweb.com, lowestfare.com, rentalcars.com, and reezenet. com. Priceline.com has also entered the market of financial services, where they offer consumers home mortgages and other loans.

In an effort to diversify their product offerings, Priceline.com acquired several businesses, enabling them to offer new products and services at lower prices. For example, in 2007, Priceline.com acquired the Agoda Company, a Bangkok and Singapore based company. The acquisition of the Agoda Company improved Priceline.com's Asia-Pacific regional presence. Agoda.com offers online hotel reservations at low prices to consumers in the Asia-Pacific region. The Priceline.com corporation has established a presence in Europe through its acquisition of Booking.com, an online company who offers hotel reservations at competitive prices to over 20 million customers.

The presence of Priceline.com in different geographic markets has forced Priceline to adapt to the protocol followed in the Asian and European markets. For example, to function efficiently in the Japanese marketplace, Priceline.com Corporation must consider various aspects of the Japanese culture. In Japanese culture, people read from right to left; therefore, Priceline.com had to design its website such that the content is written and read from right to left. In addition, Japanese custom stresses price negotiation, no matter what is being bought. As Priceline.com has very low profit margins, they must be prepared to incur short-term losses in the market. Also, the Japanese do not perceive contracts to be a final agreement, so Priceline.com needs to have provisions to adjust to re-negotiations. Priceline's website needs to have active customer service, as Japanese culture breeds an expectation of formality and Japanese customers generally will not be satisfied unless customer service is constantly available. Additionally, Japanese culture stresses the favorability of odd numbers, so Priceline must avoid offering prices that are even numbers.

CHAPTER SUMMARY

This chapter has explained the importance, meaning, and definition of protocol and the role it plays for e-businesses. This chapter has discussed the importance of Internationalization, Localization, and Culture when following a protocol. This chapter has also shown how systems and procedures are being followed by various organizations across the e-commerce landscape, and why it is important to have policies that safeguard the interests of the organization and its customers. In addition, this chapter outlined the ethical concerns, along with other related issues that affect the organization. This chapter concluded with a discussion of how businesses can prepare themselves to handle the cultural and language differences of customers across different countries.

The case study at the end provides an example of how an e-business can perform well by following protocol.

REVIEW QUESTIONS

1. Define the term Protocol and explain why it is important for an organization to follow Protocol in its operation?

2. Explain Systems and Procedures for an organization with your own example?

3. What are some of the Legal and Ethical issues that organizations should be concerned about?

4. Briefly describe the different areas of concerns an organization has with regard to Protocol?

REFERENCES

1. http://pwebs.net/marketing/ethics/articles/internetethics.htm

2. http://vocabulary-vocabulary.com/dictionary/protocol.php

3. http://www.answers.com/topic/protocol?cat=health

4. Efraim Turban, Jae Kyu Lee, Dave King, Judy McKay, Peter Marshall, *Electronic Commerce 2008*, Prentice Hall, 5th Edition; 2008.

5. Efraim Turban, David King, Jae Lee and Merrill Warkentin, "*Electronic Commerce*"2002; (Prentice Hall); ISBN 0-13-065301-2.

6. H. M. Deitel, P. J. Deitel and K.Steinbuhler, "*e-Business and e-Commerce for Managers*", Prentice-Hall, New Jersey, 2001, ISBN: 0-13-032364-0.

7. Judith C Simon, Lillian H Chaney, *Systems and Procedures for Modern Office: A Simulation Approach*, Prentice Hall.

8. http://www.webresultsinc.com/acceptableuse.htm

CHAPTER 12

PRIVACY

Chapter Contents

- Objectives
- Introduction
- Information and Information Collection
- Privacy Concerns
- Technologies
    1. Privacy Invading Technologies
        1a. Spyware
        1b. Cookies
        1c. Web Bugs

        1d. Spam
    2. Privacy Enhancing Technologies

        2a. Encryptions

        2b. P3P

        2c. Proxies and Firewall

        2d. Contracts
- Privacy Laws (Privacy Legislations)
    1. Regulatory Bodies
    2. Privacy Laws

        2.1. Electronic Communications Privacy Act

        2.2. Children Online Privacy Act.

        2.3 Gramm-Leach Bliley Act (GLB Act)

        2.4. Data Protection Act

        2.5. The German Teleservices Protection Act
- Privacy Projects

    1. PRIME

    2. Transparent Accountable Datamining Initiative
    - Chapter Review
    - Review Questions
    - References

OBJECTIVES

The objective of this chapter is to discuss the importance of privacy on the Internet. There are four types of privacy concerns which arise when there is an information trail: 1) awareness of data collections, 2) duration, 3) secondary use, and 4) degree of control. Privacy of a consumer's personal information can and must be provided through electronic means. Common information gathered on websites is one of three types: 1) anonymous information, 2) personally unidentifiable information, 3) personally identifiable information. The Federal Trade Commission (FTC) oversees the safeguarding of information privacy in the United States. Technologies like Spyware, Spam, and Cookies help to protect the invasion of privacy of Internet users. Privacy enhancing technologies like P3P and PKI enable the Internet users to increase their level of privacy when surfing the Internet.

Many countries have different laws applicable in their respective countries safeguarding their people as well. Some of these laws include the Electronic Communications Privacy Act, Personal Information Protection and Electronics Document Act (PIPEDA), Children Online Privacy Act, and Data Protection Act. For example, there are various projects on privacy being conducted by the W3C, P3P and Transparent Accountable Datamining Initiative. This chapter concludes with a case study about DoubleClick and its success in providing Internet advertising solutions and services to publishers, marketers, and agencies using rich media content, video, and other digital medium.

INTRODUCTION

Privacy is defined as the "right to be left alone", and is one of the most complex issues in Internet marketing. The last chapter explained the need for businesses to focus on privacy issues when setting their guidelines and protocols. Internet privacy is mainly concerned with consumer privacy, and it deals with the handling and protection of sensitive personal information that the consumer provides to the business electronically. Without proper protection, personal information provided by the consumer can be accessed and used for financial fraud and identity theft.

New Internet users may not realize that any message they post, transactions they conduct, and any webpages they access can be traced by third-party users. During the early stages of Internet marketing, consumers were initially concerned about the privacy of confidential information like credit card number, birth date and social security numbers. They also were uncertain about the quality of product that they would receive. Therefore, it was a slow process for consumers to shift to online shopping. Even as the shift to online shopping has occurred more dramatically, privacy concerns still remain for consumers and must be addressed by companies involved in e-business.

One recent example is the security breach in Second Life[61], an online game provider in 2006. The customer database that held unencrypted names, addresses, encrypted passwords and billing information of 650,000 users was exposed to the Internet. This breach brought monetary loss and non-monetary loss in terms of loss of reputation and trust. Privacy concerns have always existed in business, but have become even more prevalent now that confidential information is much more accessible. Privacy concerns are also an issue in the case of high profile celebrities having their photographs distributed over the Internet. The leakage of Bill Gates' photograph in jail and the exposure

---

61 www.second-life.com

of Pamela Anderson life are both examples of the invasion of privacy.

INFORMATION AND INFORMATION COLLECTION

Although many sites are not interested in the active profiling of their users, there are websites like e-Bay and Amazon that need to maintain an active interest of their user profiles to maintain competitive advantages. Profiles are made based on the information collected by the sites, whether directly or indirectly. **Direct Information** is supplied by the users, usually in the form of birth dates, security numbers, credit card details and contact details. Generally, direct information is collected using forms. **Indirect Information** is collected without direct communication from the user. The host server records information about each visit by tracking the pages visited, time spent on each page, search terms used, purchases made, and the different advertisements viewed. Another way of collecting information is through the website's banner, which allows third party advertisers to track users' browsing habits. Data collected through direct and indirect methods are used to gauge user preferences and ultimately target the sale of certain products. These methods of data collection are made possible by the availability of sophisticated technologies.

There are three types of information: anonymous information, personally unidentifiable information, personally identifiable information.

- **Anonymous Information** refers to information gathered without the use of any invasive technologies. Typical anonymous information consists of the user machine's IP address, domain type, browser version and type, operating system, and local time the customer is accessing the webpage at.

- **Personally Unidentifiable Information** consists of pieces of information like user age, date of birth, gender, country that, on their own, cannot identify an individual. Generally these pieces of information are willingly submitted by users through forms, but sometimes may be obtained through the use of tracking technology.

- **Personally Identifiable Information** consists of information that can identify an individual. Information such as email addresses, name, phone number, and credit card number fall into this category. These pieces of information are collected directly from the customer by the seller through the registration or sales process.

PRIVACY CONCERNS

Customers are the most affected by privacy concerns from online shopping. Social interaction on the Internet has become very popular. Websites that provide these social networking opportunities have little or no regard for privacy. The users are not aware of the trail of information they leave that can be found on the Internet. There are four types of privacy concerns that commonly arise for customers.

- **Awareness of Data Collections:** The extent to which customer information is collected and stored by businesses.

- **Secondary Use:** Secondary use refers to the concerns that users have about the use of their personal information for other purposes without their personal authorization. Secondary usage can happen in two ways: internal and external usage. Internal usage refers to the use of data and information inside the organization that collected the data. External usage refers to the disclosure of information to external organizations.

- **Degree of Control:** The degree of control that a business has over the collection and usage of particular customer information.

- **Duration and Extent of the Transaction:** The future use of the information stored in the database when an individual is not aware of its use is also an important privacy concern.

Concerns over the loss of privacy can now be measured with an instrument called Concern for Information Privacy (CFIP)[62], which takes into account the above mentioned features. CFIP is defined as "the expectancy of a customer to rely upon database marketers to treat the consumer's personal information fairly"[63]. It is also defined as the ability of individuals to be in control of their own personal information.

TECHNOLOGIES

Technology has made it easier to invade the privacy of the individual. E-Businesses have an incentive to use technology to gather information about their customers for profiling and marketing purposes. Technology affects the privacy of Internet users in two ways. For example, there is available technology in the form of spyware or cookies that help to invade the privacy of Internet users. In response,

---

62   J.H. Smith, S.J. Milberg and S.J. Burke(1996), Information privacy: Measuring individuals' concerns about corporate practices, MIS Quarterly 20(2), 167-196.
63   Culnan, M.J., & Armstrong, P.K. (1999). Information privacy concerns, procedural fairness, and impersonal trust: An empirical investigation. *Organization Science, 10*(1), 104-115.

Internet users can use technology like P3P and PKI, which enhance the level of privacy that Internet users can experience while browsing the Internet. These technologies were developed to provide protection when checking e-mail. They are especially effective when using the Internet for purposes of online shopping. Law enforcement agencies like the FBI depend on privacy invading technology to track cyber criminals.

1. Privacy Invading Technologies

1a. Spyware

Spyware is a program which remains on a person's computer to secretly gather information and relay it to the interested party. The way spyware enters a person's computer is either as a software virus or as some kind of attachment to a new program that a user downloads or installs. Generally, spyware is installed either through a download or through pop up windows without the user's consent. For these reasons, spyware programs are generally known as "Potentially unwanted programs" (PUP). Cookies and Web Bugs are the mechanisms through which spyware is installed on the user's computer.

Yahoo, a global internet service provider, has been criticized for funding spyware and adware. Yahoo provides services like web-portals, search engines, e-mail, news, and discussion forums. Yahoo clients post their pop-ups on Yahoo's websites, and the Yahoo users may unknowingly install spyware on their computer.

1b. Cookies

Cookies are software codes that can collect and store information like the user's name, password, user IP address, and tracking of the user's web activity. Cookies are generally used as digital identifier tags by the vendors and are generally found on the hard drive. Cookies are found in the HTTP headers and have 5 parameters in their code: 1) the name, 2) value, 3) expiration date, 4) domain, and 5) secure connection. However, the users can configure their web browser to disable cookies.

Cookies through HTTP headers, are stored in the memory of a computer's browser. Even when the computer is shut off, the cookies are still active in the hard drive. Every time the browser is opened by the user, the cookies are read from the disk and every time the browser is closed, the cookies are saved on the hard drive.

1c. Web Bugs

Web Bugs are images embedded in webpages and HTML-formatted emails. With the size of one pixel in width and height, they are generally invisible. They are also known as 'clear GIF', '1-by-1 GIFs' and 'invisible GIF'. A web bug is used to find whether a particular e-mail message has been read. Web bugs also provide the IP address of the computer, URL of the page, time, and the type of browser that viewed the page. Web bugs are used by the advertising networks, either in their webpages or mass e-mails, to update and edit information about personal profiles stored in cookies and to collect statistics about the number of visits a site receives.

A web bug is found by viewing the HTML code of a webpage and searching for IMG tag. An example is shown below (Figure 1).

Example of Web Bugs found in Quicken's home page
(www.quicken.com):

<img src="http://ad.doubleclick.net/ad/pixel.quicken/
NEW" width=1 height=1 border=0>

<IMG WIDTH=1 HEIGHT=1 border=0 SRC="http://
media.preferences.com/ping?ML_SD=IntuitTE_
Intuit_1x1_RunOfSite_Any &db_afcr=4B31-
C2FB-10E2C&event=reghome&group=register&
time=1999.10.27.20.5 6.37">

The two Web Bugs were placed on the home page by Quicken to provide "hit" information about visitors to DoubleClick and MatchLogic (AKA, preferences.com), two Internet advertising companies.

Figure 1: Example of Web Bugs found in Quicken's homepage

1d. Spam
Spam is a collection of unsolicited bulk messages sent to a group of email recipients and is the most common and recognized form of e-business privacy invasion. Generally, e-commerce users who have purchased products over the Internet, have participated in newsgroups or mailing lists, or subscribed to a particular website and receive junk e-mail get invaded in the form of Spam. People who send out spam are known as spammers.

The most popular form of spamming is video spamming. Other forms of spamming are web search engine spam, usenet newsgroup spam, spam in blogs, wiki spam, junk fax transmissions, and Internet forum. One of the biggest disadvantages of spam, apart from invasion to privacy, is that it slows down the whole network. However, it is the least costly form of advertising for businesses. Spam requires little to no operating costs for advertisers, allowing them to advertise its products on a large scale through e-mails, blogs and social networking groups.

2. Privacy Enhancing Technologies
2a. Encryptions

To have secure e-commerce transactions, encryptions are required. **Encryption** is the conversion of data to ciphertext, which is not easily understood by unauthorized people. Once the ciphertext is transmitted or accessed, it is then converted again into its original form. This process is called a decryption.

In e-commerce, the most common encryption approach is through public key infrastructure. The PKI allows users to use the Internet for a secure exchange of money through the use of a cryptographic key. For secure use of e-mail, organizations use "pretty good privacy" (PGP), which allows an individual to encrypt his message so that the message cannot be tampered with en route. It is generally used in anonymous remailer's technology, where the sender's address is assigned a fake address by the server. This technology was created in 1997. It started as Type 0, where one operator had control over the anonymity of the e-mail users. To address multiple operators, Type 1 was developed and later yielded to a more sophisticated Type II.

2b. P3P

Platform for Privacy Preferences or **P3P** project, is a protocol that allows different websites to establish a standard format for their privacy practices. This was developed by the World-Wide-Web Consortium for the purpose of giving more control to the users over their personal information. A P3P compliant website declares the type of information it will collect and how it will use the information. Websites using P3P standards make their practices explicit, exposing them to public scrutiny and enabling users to understand and appreciate those privacy standards. Customer demand for privacy settings gives e-commerce sites a strong incentive to implement measures that protect the privacy of customers. Netscape 7 and Internet Explorer 7 have privacy-related features that are based on P3P standards.

Privacy Policy deals with the types of information that the e-business stores, the intended use of this information, the duration of the storage of the information, and the accessibility of the information for third parties. P3P is designed such that it is integrated into the browsers, thereby enabling the users to manage their personal information across multiple websites. However, P3P is facing a dilemma as to whether it should share information automatically to the vendors, or if customers should have to approve of the information sharing.

2c. Proxies and Firewalls

Proxies and **Firewalls** are barriers between a computer and the Internet, restricting the types of communications that take place. Communications generally takes place through third party software. Third party software uses anonymizing features that directs the browsing of the Internet through an intermediary provider. This helps to prevent unauthorized parties from gathering personal information. Software has also been developed that enables a computer to block communications such as junk e-mail, ad banners, or other types of privacy-invading software. Computers that have these measures implemented are known as proxy computers.

Firewalls can be controlled by users based on their preferences. For example, rules can be set to block all cookies from a specified domain or e-mail server. The 4 best types of firewall software are Checkpoint's Zone Alarm Pro, Comodo Firewall Pro, Sunbelt Personal Firewall, and Tall Amu Online Armor. These firewall software options provide high security for Internet users. Newer computers generally come equipped with firewall software.

2d. Contracts

Contracts, with respect to privacy, are tools enabling the customers and sellers to make their own rules based on the types of transactions and services being exchanged. The seller promises to keep the customer data secret, even at a monetary loss. If the seller reveals the secret, the customer has the right to sue the seller. However, given that these are electronic agreements, the electronic document and promise is the only thing that binds both parties to the contract. Upon breach of contract, customers can file a class-action suit and ask regulatory bodies like the Federal Trade Commission (FTC) to act on their behalf. The scandal associated with a lawsuit can bring significant damage to the reputation of e-businesses. However, contracts are limited in that they only affect the contracting parties. If the information is inadvertently leaked, it is a breach of the privacy contract. However, the customer cannot sue the company that is not a party to the contract who has accessed the data through the first company.

Labeling and **Filtering** technology also provide means to promoting fair information practices on the Internet. This technology also assures compliance with various national data protection laws. The platform for Internet Content Selection, or PICS, is an example of this technology. Based on HTML protocol, PICS was designed to help parents control the websites that their children can view by allowing selective blocking of the content on the Internet. The protocol defines a standard format for rating labels. These rating labels evaluate the content of a site and the software is so designed that it filters the labels that are evaluated to not be appropriate for children.

PRIVACY LAWS

The information that is generally available online allows other vendors to collect relevant information about consumers to construct more accurate consumer profiles. A recent report from the FTC observes that, although the information gathered by network advertisers is often anonymous (i.e. the profiles are linked to the identification number of the advertising network's cookie on the consumer's computer rather than the name of a specific person), in some cases, the profiles derived from tracking consumers' activities on the web are linked or merged with personally identifiable information. This consumer data can also be combined with data on the consumer's offline purchases, or information collected directly from consumers through surveys and registration forms[64].

1. Regulatory Bodies

Internet crime, especially in data theft, has escalated over time. This has led to more laws designed to address and therefore, to address various aspects of privacy invasion and data theft. However, as consumers are unable to keep track of whether their personal information has been released to unauthorized sources while shopping online, enforcement responsibility for Internet crime falls on government agencies and **Regulatory Bodies**. Each country has its own sets of regulatory bodies that ensure that privacy laws are enforced in a precise and efficient manner. The role of a regulatory agency is to protect the public from cyber theft and crime.

The Federal Trade Commission (FTC) enforces information privacy laws in the United States. The FTC has provided a set of guidelines, known as the Fair Information Practices, which incorporate rules that define the processes of collecting information, rectifying errors, informing the customers while collecting information, and prevention of unauthorized access to information. The guidelines take into account five principal actions: 1) disclosure notices, 2) choice on how to disclose information, 3) access to information to exercise control, 4) mechanisms to be employed to protect consumer information, and finally, and 5) enforcing sanctions for potential violations. The FTC has more tightly regulated with respect to Internet commerce privacy concerns and continues to monitor privacy problems.

---

64   Please see http://www.ftc.gov/os/2000/07/onlineprofiling.htm

2. Privacy Laws

The advances of the Internet has led to a more globally linked world and has increased data flow across countries, contributing to the problems of information privacy on the Internet. **Privacy Laws** developed by various countries have the same implications but may be enforced in different ways. Laws such as the Personal Information Protection and Electronics Document Act (PIPEDA) in Canada, Children's Online Privacy Protection Act (COPPA), Health Insurance Portability and Protection Act (HIPAA) and The Grahamm-Leach Bailey Act (GLB Act) in the United States, and the Data Protection Directive in the European Union allow organizations to prosecute criminals in cases of misuse of data. The Department of Justice in the United States has subpoenaed the search engines websites Google, AOL, Yahoo and MSN for certain data practices. Google refused to comply with the DOJ, citing that it is too burdensome to go through each log because of the high quantity of data involved. Currently, they are involved in a lawsuit against the DOJ. However, the other major search engines, Yahoo, AOL and MSN complied with the request. This shows the power of the government to regulate companies to maintain the privacy of information on the Internet.

2.1. Electronic Communications Privacy Act

The **Electronic Communications Privacy Act** (ECPA) imposes civil and criminal penalties for the disclosure, use, and interception of electronic communications. The Personal Information Protection and Electronics Document Act (PIPEDA) came into effect in April 2000 and protects personal information that is collected, used or disclosed. This act was designed to support and promote e-commerce in Canada.

2.2. Children Online Privacy Protection Act

The **Children Online Privacy Protection Act** came into effect in 1998 to safeguard the interests of children under the age of 13. It is a United States federal law and deals with online child pornography. Its website, www.coppa.org, defines and details important terms. In addition, the website shows the rules regarding the responsibilities of an operator of websites and online services. The FTC has already fined website operators for their failure to comply with COPPA requirements. Some of the websites that have incurred fines are Hershey Foods, Mrs. Field's Cookies and American Pop Corn Company. Xanga, a New York based website that hosts web logs, photo logs, and offers social networking profiles, has already been fined $1 million USD for not complying with COPPA standards. Xanga violated the COPPA by allowing children under the age of 13 to repeatedly sign up for services without requiring parental consent.

2.3. Gramm-Leach Bliley Act (GLB Act)

The **Gramm-Leach Bliley Act**; also known as the Financial Modernization Act of 1999, protects consumers' personal financial information held by financial institutions. The act consists of financial privacy rules, safeguard of information rules and gives authority to eight federal agencies and states to enforce these rules. This act applies to banks, securities firms, insurance companies and other companies involved in financial services. In addition, the act governs the collection and disclosure of customers' personal financial information by financial institutions. The act also ensures the protection of customer information. This rule is applied not only to financial institutions that collect information from their own customers, but also to financial institutions that receive customer information from other financial institutions.

2.4. Data Protection Act

The **Data Protection Act** defines a legal basis for the handling of cases related to the protection of personal data in the United Kingdom. It was created in 1984 and now also is enforced in other European Union member countries. The act provides individuals with a certain set of principles about how personal information is collected, the type of personal data collected and how a person's rights can be protected. The act provides specific guidelines for information retrieval by the individual himself, release of personal information without consent, and the time period that businesses may keep personal information. The office of the Information Commissioner oversees the enforcement of this act. In addition, the Information Commissioner develops and maintains the guidelines that are related to this act.

2.5. The German Teleservices Protection Act

The **German Teleservices Protection Act** was passed in 1997 and was designed to address the privacy and data protection issues that arise in the Internet context. It was enacted as federal data protection legislation for Germany. It provides protection to Internet users by making it mandatory for service providers to assign anonymous and pseudonymous use of payment services. This act also prohibits the storing and use of user profiles unless they are assigned pseudonymous names. It also addresses other issues, like the processing of clickstream data and transactional anonymity.

PRIVACY PROJECTS

There are many ongoing research projects designed to address privacy concerns in the e-business marketplace.

1. PRIME

Privacy and Identity Management for Europe, **PRIME**, is a research project funded by European Union's Sixth Framework Program and the Swiss Federal Office for Education and Science. Its aim is to develop a working prototype of a privacy-enhancing identity management system that will help to make it easy to for users to decide what data to make available on the Internet. PRIME requires the contribution of experts in the fields of service provision, along with academic and data protection authorities. PRIME is a system supporting the development of European privacy regulations.

2. Transparent Accountable Datamining Initiative

The **Transparent Accountable Datamining Initiative,** otherwise known as the TAMI project, is funded by the National Science Foundation (NSF) and is implemented by the Decentralized Information Group (DIG)[65]. TAMI creates technical, legal, and policy foundations for transparency and accountability for information systems. It is critical, especially in the web domain, to incorporate transparency as it helps to manage privacy risks that are incurred due to communications, search, and storage technology. In addition, TAMI analyzes the risks of privacy protection and helps to increase the reliability of data aggregation. The project is geared towards developing precise rule languages that help to clearly express the different policy constraints. The rule language also enables the reasoning engines to describe the results.

---

65 DIG is based at MIT's Computer Science and Artificial Intelligence Laboratory. It is led by Eim Berners-Lee, inventor of World Wide Web. It works closely with World Wide Web Consortium (W3C).

CASE STUDY

DoubleClick is a company that provides Internet advertising solutions and services to publishers, marketers, and agencies that use rich media contents, video, and other digital mediums. It was founded in 1995 as Internet Advertising Network by Kevin O'Connor and Dwight Merriman. In 1996, it was renamed as DoubleClick after its acquisition by Poppe-Tyson. DoubleClick is located in New York and now has 17 offices and development centers around the world. In addition, DoubleClick has 15 data centers which are located around the world. DoubleClick has more than 1200 employees around the world. It was one of the first dot.com companies to venture into the online media representation business. DoubleClick's client base includes multinationals like Microsoft, General Motors, Nike and Coca-Cola, who use the internet advertising services of DoubleClick.

DoubleClick began its product portfolio by offering online ad serving and management technology under the portfolio of DART services. The current product portfolio includes DART Search, Motif (Rich Media) and DoubleClick Advertising Exchange, all of which are offered to both publishers and advertisers. The integrated products help the company to manage advertising sales, buying, operations, and billings. DoubleClick helps the company to succeed in Internet marketing by providing high quality digital media. It also helps in providing banners, videos and display ads to promote a business.

In 2007, Google agreed to acquire DoubleClick for 3.1 billion dollars. This move enables Google to enter the business of advertising. The acquisition raises concerns among privacy and antitrust advocates on the potential monopoly and privacy issues. The acquisition was approved by both FTC and European Union regulators thus allaying the fears among consumers about the privacy of information.

DoubleClick uses two types of cookies: 1) persistent and 2) session, in their website to collect information. The **Persistent Cookie** enters the web browser of the consumer and stays even when the computer is shut down. The **Session Cookies** are held temporarily in the computer's memory and disappear when the browser is closed. They also use web beacons or pixel tags with the cookies. The banner ad of their products has session cookies in place that allows the marketing people to assess the popularity and effectiveness of ads. DoubleClick claims that the information collected by session cookies is not used to send e-mails about future goods and services. It ensures that e-mails about products and other offerings are sent to only those consumers who have filled out their subscription form.

DoubleClick has implemented many security measures to protect personal and non-personal information. Information such as contact or business details are deleted after a specified period of time so that they are not accessible later to the employee. It can also be deleted on request by the concerned party. The company has taken strict steps against employees who misuse and alter private information about the consumers. Double Click is now certified for European Union-United States Safe Harbor program, which protects the European visitors against privacy issues.

DoubleClick follows different privacy compliant policies to ensure consumer privacy. It has disclosed the process of information collection and has taken full responsibility of information confidentiality. Apart from this, it has become Network Advertising Initiative compliant. It also has the license of the TRUSTe[66] Privacy program. As a TRUSTe licensee, the information practices and privacy practices have to be compliant with Network Advertising Initiative. Being NAI compliant requires DoubleClick to disclose the type of personally-identifiable information collected, sharing and usage of information, and the security procedures in place to protect the loss and misuse of information the company collects.

CHAPTER SUMMARY

Internet privacy, better known as consumer privacy, deals with the handling and protection of sensitive personal information that the consumer provides through electronic means. Profiles are made by the company based on the information collected on their website and any additional information found on other websites. The information is collected directly or indirectly, in the form of: 1) anonymous information, 2) personally unidentifiable information, and 3) personally identifiable information.

There are four types of privacy concerns which arise from the trail of information left on the Internet: 1) awareness of data collections, 2) duration, 3) secondary use, and 4) degree of control. Technologies such as Spyware, Spam, Cookies, etc. invade the privacy of Internet users. Privacy enhancing technologies such as P3P, PKI, enable the Internet users to increase their level of privacy when surfing the Internet.

The Federal Trade Commission (FTC) enforces and safeguards consumer information privacy in the United States. Different countries are governed by different laws. Some of these laws include

---

66 TRUSTe is an independent, non-profit organization whose mission is to build trust and confidence in the Internet by promoting the use of fair information practices.

the Electronic Communications Privacy Act, Personal Information Protection and Electronics Document Act (PIPEDA), Children Online Privacy Act, and Data Protection Act. In addition, there are various projects on privacy being conducted by the W3C, P3P and Transparent Accountable Datamining Initiative.

REVIEW QUESTIONS

1. What is consumer privacy? Why is it important for the websites to maintain consumer privacy?
2. How is information to develop visitor profiles collected?
3. What are the different privacy concerns? How do you measure the concern for invasion to privacy?
4. How is technology used to help to address consumer privacy?
5. Explain the different technologies that help to protect consumer privacy.
6. How is consumer privacy enforced in different countries?
7. A website in Europe was involved in data theft. The users of that website wanted to file a suit against that company. What are the different laws that the users can use to help them file a suit?
8. Is there any law that helps to protect the privacy of the children?
9. Who regulates the privacy law in the United State?
10. Describe the various privacy projects undertaken by W3C?

REFERENCES

1. A.D. Miyazaki and A. Fernandez, Internet privacy and security: An examination of online retailer disclosures, *Journal of Public Policy & Marketing* 19(1) (2000) 54–61.
2. Bygrave, Lee (1998); Germany's Teleservices Data Protection

Act; Privacy law and Policy reporter 5, 53-54.

3. Chellapa, R and Sin, R(20005), Personalization Versu Privacy: An Empirical Examination of the Online Consumer's Dilemma, Information Technology and Management 6, 181-202.

4. Cookie; accessed on 16-3-2008; http://www.cookiecentral. com/faq/

5. COPPA; http://www.coppa.org/coppa.htm

6. Culnan, M.J., & Armstrong, P.K. (1999). Information privacy concerns, procedural fairness, and impersonal trust: An empirical investigation. Organization Science, 10(1), 104-115.

7. D. Gillin, The federal trade commission and Internet privacy, Marketing Research 12(3) (2000) 39.

8. Data Protection Act; http://www.opsi.gov.uk/Acts/acts1998/ ukpga_19980029_en_1

9. K.A. Stewart and A.H. Segars, An empirical examination of the concern for information privacy instrument, Information Systems Research 13(1) (2002) 36–49.

10. Firewall; http://www.firewallguide.com/

11. Karat, C. Blom, J, Karat, J (2004); Designing Personalized User Experience in E-Commerce, Publisher; Springer.

12. PIPIEPDA; http://www.privcom.gc.ca/ legislation/02_06_01_01_e.asp

13. PRIME; accessed on 14-3-2008; https://www.prime-project. eu/about/factsheet/

14. http://www.ftc.gov/privacy/privacyinitiatives/glbact.html

15. Second life; http://www.secondlife.com/

16. SPAM; official site of Spam; accessed on 16-3-2008; http:// www.spam.com/legal/spam/

17. Stone, E.F., Gardner, D.G., Guetal, H.G., & McClure, S.

(1983). A field experiment comparing information-privacy values, beliefs, and attitudes across several types of organizations. *Journal of Applied Psychology,* 68(3), 459-468.

18. Shim, J.T., Slyek, C.V (2004); *Does Trust reduce concern for information privacy in E-commerce?* http://sais.aisnet. org/2004/.%5CShim,%20VanSlyke,%20Jiang%20&%20 Johnson.pdf

19. Smith, Richard (1999); Web bugs; accessed on 14-3-2008; http://w2.eff.org/Privacy/Marketing/web_bug.html

20. Smith, J.H, S.J. Milberg and S.J. Burke (1996), Information privacy: Measuring individuals' concerns about corporate practices, MIS Quarterly 20(2), 167-196.

21. TAMI; accessed on 14-3-2008; http://dig.csail.mit.edu/ TAMI/

22. www.doubleclick.com

23. http://www.privacychoices.org/understanding.htm

24. Holahan, Catherine, Google's DoubleClick Strategic move; Published on April 17, 2007, Businessweek, accessed on May 1, 2008; http://www.businessweek.com/technology/content/ apr2007/tc20070414_675511.htm

25. Volokh, Eugene (2000); Personalization and Privacy; Communications of the Association for Computing Machinery 43(8).

CHAPTER 13

CONCLUSION

Chapter Contents

- Introduction
- Importance of each P in Successful Contemporary Marketing
- Nurturing the 11 Ps for Successful Marketing

INTRODUCTION

The advancement of digital technology and widespread Internet access have drastically changed the dynamics of marketing in the global marketplace. The traditional 4 Ps of marketing, while still applicable, are no longer sufficient for both traditional businesses and e-businesses. The contemporary marketing mix should include additional 7 Ps. Each additional P plays an integral role for businesses to understand and meet the needs and preferences of their customers. The 11 Ps, altogether, enable marketers to gather important customer information, and to use this information to make more personalized product offerings and provide better overall customer service. This contemporary marketing mix not only attracts new customers more easily, but also creates long-term relationships with repeat customers due to the higher quality of service provided. In addition, utilization of the 11 Ps makes important information available to both sides of the business – the seller and customers, which leads to more informed decisions on product offerings and purchases.

IMPORTANCE OF EACH P IN SUCCESSFUL CONTEMPORARY MARKETING

E-Marketing has become so common today that it is impossible to think of marketing without involving digital technology. The term 'e' from 'e-marketing' is slowly vanishing because of the common use of digital and Internet technology. In the near future, there will likely be no distinction between "e-marketing" and marketing because the Internet has become such a fundamental part of marketing plans for all businesses. Each of the 11 Ps plays an important role in the successful implementation of a marketing strategy.

With the continuous technological advancements, it would be not surprising to see further expansion of the Ps, and subsequently the 11 Ps will become insufficient in the future. Technological changes require marketers to constantly re-evaluate their marketing methods and look to integrate newer technology successfully into their marketing strategies. In the current marketplace, the 11 Ps represent a complete and successful marketing model: People, Product, Partnership, Productivity, Price, Place, Promotion, Personalization, Physical Image, Protocol, and Privacy.

IMPORTANCE OF EACH P FOR SUCCESS OF CONTEMPORARY MARKETING MIX

1) People: Despite all of the technological changes, the target audience for marketers is still People. People have different preferences that must be met in the online shopping environment, and thus must be an important consideration of a contemporary marketing strategy.

2) Product: Today's products can be sold more effectively by marketers who use Internet technology to display and promote products in an attractive manner to their target audience. Marketers are concentrating more on extending the growth and the maturity stages of the Product Life Cycle in an effort to maximize profit on each product offering.

3) Partnership: Partnerships are the strategic alliances that businesses form to optimize their competitiveness in the marketplace. Partnerships help to provide better customer service, superior planning and product offerings, and more efficient supply and distribution of products. E-Partnerships are agreements formed over the Internet between two or more organizations to fulfill a set of goals previously agreed for mutual benefit. The organizations involved in these alliances remain independent but assist each other by providing each other with necessary services, including products, supply and distribution services, additional manufacturing capacity, etc. Once a partnership is formed, the e-business partners share the accompanying risks, losses, and profits. A partnership can be formed through Forward Alliances or Backward Alliances. A forward alliance is formed through licensing, franchising, and royalties. A backward alliance is formed through joint ventures, strategic alliances and contract manufacturing. A partnership is successful only when the partners share an understanding of each others' business models and objectives. There are three stages of partnership formation: 1) Initial Stage, 2) Intensive Stage, and 3) the Dissolution Stage. The Initial Stage involves strategy formation and partner identification. The Intensive Stage involves the negotiation stage, commitment stage and execution stage. The final stage is the Dissolution Stage, which involves the termination of the partnership.

4) Productivity: The usage of information technology and increasing channels of communication have increased the potential output for all organizations, thus contributing to the increase of productivity. Although productivity can be affected by many factors, including technological development, economic conditions, and other exogenous issues, marketers must keep all relevant productivity considerations in mind while forming and adjusting their marketing strategies. Productivity is also dependent on the effective use of organizational resources, such as physical capital, human capital, inventory, and monetary funds.. To maximize productivity, businesses must maintain best efforts to effectively manage productivity determinants within their control while responding effectively to any adverse events outside of their control.

5) Price: Marketers today pay very close attention to the pricing strategies of their products, due to the high price elasticity in the current marketplace. Customers are very sensitive to slight differences in price for similar products. Pricing strategies, to a great extent, depend on market conditions. Moreover, the widespread accessibility of information makes the pricing game more difficult for marketers, as customers are immediately alerted of superior prices and are willing to buy from competitors.

6) Place: Strategies for distribution and Supply Chain Management have changed since the development of the Internet. Fast and efficient delivery is the main priority now for e-businesses. Place refers to the usage of the Internet in the placement, logistics, and distribution of products and services. In the virtual environment, a company's website is where product distribution takes place. Supply Chain Management teams traditionally handle a company's logistics and product distribution. The Internet has made product placement and distribution easier for e-businesses. The components of place for e-enabled business are e-commerce, e-procurement and e-collaboration. E-procurement and e-collaboration form the back end of the business and are used to handle most of the processes typically handled by the traditional supply chain management team. E-Commerce is the front end of the business, where customers browse the company's website to buy desired products. E-Commerce refers to the transactions conducted over the Internet in the following markets: business-to-business (B2B), consumer to consumer (C2C), business-to-consumer (B2C), and consumer-to-business (C2B). E-procurement refers to online transactions between various suppliers. E-Informing, e-tendering, ERP and E-MRO are all different types of e-procurement processes. E-Collaboration refers to the collaboration between individuals and businesses via electronic tools, such as e-mail and video conferencing.

7) Promotion: The Internet's popularity has led a majority of businesses to re-vamp their operations and establish an Internet presence. Some businesses use the Internet to procure supplies, while others sell their own products online. Businesses have used the Internet in an effort to forego meaningful customer relationships, promote specific product offerings, and increase online and offline sales. In all cases, businesses have found it difficult to forego the opportunities for business growth and expansion that come from the Internet. Gradually, businesses started exploring the Internet with different types of messages to a targeted audience. They began with "banner ads", ads placed on a webpage with a link for customers to go to the advertiser's promotional page. Banner ads were followed by e-mail advertising, links on complementary sites, search engine advertising, viral strategies, and many other forms of advertising. Advertisers found the Internet an effective medium due to the benefits that they can monitor the effectiveness of their advertising methods and the appeal of their products. Online promotional technology has improved greatly with the introduction of rich media, which has made ads more interactive and more appealing to many different types of customers. Advertisers have greatly benefited from the low cost and overall effectiveness of Internet promotions. However, one thing they should always be alert on is cyber crimes and privacy issues and make efforts to maintain the security of their websites.

8) Personalization: Personalization refers to the practice of individualizing marketing content and programs for one customer based on the customer's unique profile. Personalization enables marketers to better achieve one of their most important objectives, which is to optimize customer satisfaction during their use of the company's website. Some of the personalized services that are offered include personal webpages, recommendation area, wish lists, e-mail notifications and one-click technology. A customer profile is obtained from a history of previous sessions and data provided by the customer. The different phases of personalization include customer interactions, customer profiles, analysis, additional customer data, and the targeting of marketing activities to suit the customer profile. User profiles are built by using neural networks, collaborative filtering, expert and rule based engines, forms, and clickstream analysis. Privacy is a major concern in the personalization process, however, it has been addressed by the Personalization Consortium. The Personalization Consortium is an international advocacy group that addresses the need for privacy and security in Internet marketing.

9) Physical Image: Many organizations attempt to replicate their brick-and-mortar stores through their websites. Providing a physical image to the online stores can be beneficial to the business as it helps to attract more customers and thereby generate more revenue. However, there are inherent limitations in the attempt to re-create an in-person shopping experience online. The replication approach may not be the best approach for organizations. However, it is still important for organizations to provide features online equivalent to those of in-person shopping experience. For example, organizations can provide extensive online catalogues of product offerings to simulate the experience of a physical store. Furthermore, organizations can provide graphics and more interactive features of the products, giving customers the perception of some degree of interaction. While these efforts may not fully re-create the in-store experience, they make it possible for customers to purchase more comfortably without ever setting foot inside a store.

Online shopping cart abandonment remains a challenge for e-business. Shoppers need information on the prices of various products prior to going through the checkout process. Many businesses have failed at this stage because they lacked the effective shopping cart software during their initial design of their websites. The online store must provide convenience to customers in every phase of the purchasing process. This includes product information, readily available pricing information, and a safe and secure payment process with acceptable delivery options. Therefore, while re-creating the physical image of the store can be helpful, marketers must be mindful to meet the needs of their customers first and foremost.

10) Protocol: A company's website is accessible by people all over the world via the Internet. This means that e-businesses must be aware of their presence in foreign countries and the consequent need to comply with the rules and regulations of these countries. This requires organizations to be prepared to deal with many different legal systems and specific rules. In addition, organizations must establish protocol systems that standardize the necessary procedures for not only their company but any partners or customers accessing their website. Each company generally has a policy that dictates what norms and policies are expected to be adhered to by the relevant regulatory authorities. On one hand, Internet technology has resulted in faster product cycle time, which results in lower costs and greater access to information. On the other hand, this also calls for more updated rules and guidelines to comply with worldwide rules and regulations.

11) Privacy: Privacy concerns generally revolve around consumer privacy issues. Confidential consumer information includes social security numbers, sensitive payment information, and other personal information submitted to a company's website in the form of user profiles. Consumers must feel secure that their personal information remains confidential if they disclose it to the company over the Internet; otherwise, they will not have the requisite trust needed to make online purchases. There are four types of privacy concerns which commonly arise: 1) awareness of data collections, 2) duration, 3) secondary use, and 4) degree of control. Customer profiles are developed from information collected either directly or indirectly from customers. The types of information that are disclosed can be classified into three types: a) anonymous information, b) personally unidentifiable information, c) personally identifiable information. There are such technologies as spyware, spam, and cookies that can be used to invade the privacy of Internet users. In response, softwares have been developed, such as P3P and PKI that enable Internet users to better protect themselves against privacy invasive measures. Countries have instituted various regulations to safeguard customer privacy information. A few of the privacy acts that are discussed are the Electronic Communications Privacy Act, Personal Information Protection and Electronics Document Act (PIPEDA), Children Online Privacy Act, and Data Protection Act. Long-term business growth in large part depends on the privacy policy maintained by e-marketers. Without reliable privacy measures, customers will not continue to make online purchases at the risk of their confidential information being compromised.

NURTURING 11 Ps FOR SUCCESSFUL MARKETING

Each of the 11 Ps can serve a valuable marketing purpose. It is up to the e-marketer to utilize these marketing tactics in the appropriate fashion to achieve the company's marketing objectives. This requires an understanding of the context and circumstances of the specific company within its market. Both traditional organizations and e-businesses can be well served by using the 11 Ps. However, depending on the specific situation, each company may require a greater emphasis on one P as opposed to another. Although there is no clear formula to the utilization of the 11 Ps, it is clear that in the age of Internet business, organizations must recognize the potential growth that can result from online presence. The Internet has greatly increased competitiveness amongst businesses in the marketplace, and the success of most businesses may depend on their effective utilization of information technology incorporating the 11 Ps into their marketing strategy.